CHRIS TARRANT

TARRANT ON TOP OF THE WORLD

IN SEARCH OF THE POLAR BEAR

CHRIS TARRANT

TARRANT ON TOP OF THE WORLD

IN SEARCH OF THE POLAR BEAR

WEIDENFELD & NICOLSON

Contents

Preface 6

Introduction 16

1 BASE CAMP

Longyearbyen 24

The Gun Shop 32

Barentsburg 38

Ny-Ålesund 44

The Most Northerly Man on the Planet 52

Stalking the Caribou 58

2 IN SEARCH OF THE POLAR BEAR

Turning the Ship Around 64

Icebergs 72

Bear from the Air 82

The Trapper 86

Erik and Hilda 94

The Bear in the Sea 100

3 IN THE KINGDOM OF THE POLAR BEAR

Bears Swimming 106

Bears Catching Their Food 110

Bears Feasting 120

The Walrus 126

Mother and Baby 132

Hunting Polar Bears 140

The Governor's Office 146

The Last Two Deaths 152

The Future of the Polar Bear 154

Acknowledgements 160

Preface

I found there were many encounters to be had near the top of the world. Some were intriguing, some hilarious, some downright amazing. But throughout what came to be an astonishing journey, there was one creature, present or just out of sight, who dominated everything.

The Lapps call him God's dog or the old man in the fur cloak. The Norwegians and the Danes call him the Isbjorn, or ice bear. To the Siberian tribe of the Ket, who worship all bears, he is Jyp or Grandfather. In the nineteenth century, whalers always referred to him as 'the Father'. Among Norse poets he was described as 'the rider of the iceberg' or 'the seals' dread'.

There is no doubting the beauty of these creatures, nor the terror they've inspired.

In Greenland he is Tornassuk – the master of helping spirits. To the Inuit he is Nanuk, the animal most deserving of respect.

Beliy medfet, meaning 'white bear', is the polar bear's Russian name. The Norse poets also called him 'the white sea deer', and celebrated him as having 'the strength of twelve men and the width of eleven'.

There is no doubting the beauty of these creatures, nor the terror they've inspired, largely by their formidable size. A polar bear's coat, evolved for camouflage, can vary from pure white to creamy yellow, depending on the season and the angle of the light. Sometimes oxidation from the sun can make the bear's fur look yellow or even a light brown. Though females only average 6 to 8 feet long and tend to weigh no more than 400 or 500 pounds, the adult males are the largest of all land carnivores and grow to two or even three times as large. These huge creatures can be anything between 9 and 10 feet in body length, weighing up to 1,700 pounds or, if you like, achieving the size of ten men. The biggest polar bear ever recorded was a male of 2,209 pounds in weight, who measured 12 feet long.

Polar bears have been around for about one hundred thousand years and are the top predator in the Arctic marine ecosystem. They appear to

A polar bear with lowered head is generally regarded as a sure sign of aggression. It is too late to run...

have evolved during the Pleistocene age. Like many other species the polar bears of that time were much larger than their modern descendants. Scientists believe they are descended from a group of brown bears that became isolated by glaciers near the area of northern Siberia. In order to survive on the sea ice the stranded bears underwent a rapid series of evolutionary changes. Compared to their grizzly bear cousins they have sharper teeth, and shorter and more solid claws that make them better suited for walking on ice or climbing up steep banks of snow. They also have a different shape from other members of the bear family, with much longer bodies and slender necks. Further proof that polar bears developed from an ancestral brown bear is that in areas where the two species overlap, when crossbred they produce fertile offspring.

In the poetry of the Inuit the polar bear is Pihoqahiak, which means the ever-wandering one. Though they don't mark their territory, the bears each have a home range, which varies among individuals depending on access to food and a mate. They tend to remain in the same area during any one season. But each bear's territory can change, mainly because of alterations in the sea ice itself and hence in the supply of food, especially the ringed seal. Some huge ranges have been observed, particularly in the Bering and Chukchic seas, where they may each cover up to 135,000 square miles.

Polar bears can travel as much as 20 miles a day, for several days at a time. The distances covered by polar bears are far greater than the range of any other bear species. One individual was tracked while covering more than 50 miles in twenty-four hours. Another was recorded as having travelled nearly 700 miles in a single year.

The bears prefer to travel on sea ice, and they are most abundant in those areas of ice that are broken up by each changing season. In summer they mostly stay within the southern limit of the melting ice. Sometimes they come ashore at certain established retreats, where luckily they tend to stay near the coast. But they have been sighted 100 miles or more inland when a shortage of food has forced them to travel away from the sea. During the summer months they can live mainly on the fat stored within their own body. But to survive in extreme cases the polar bear will become omnivorous, for example extending his diet by diving for seaweed or ransacking human garbage.

Above left: Polar bears have a thick layer of blubber under the skin which together with dense fur insulates them from the extreme cold.

Below left: They have shorter and more solid claws than their grizzly bear cousins, evolved for walking on ice or climbing snow banks.

Just about every aspect of a bear's existence is aimed at hunting and saving energy. Polar bears are perfectly built for the savage terrain in which they have to live, feed and breed, in northern Alaska, and in many parts of Canada, Russia, Greenland and Norway. These areas are always bitterly cold, with winter temperatures as low as minus 55 degrees Celsius, and wind speeds of up to 30 miles an hour. To help it swim, often tirelessly for long periods, the polar bear's legs are large and stocky. The feet are five-toed paws that can act like snow shoes, spreading the bear's weight as it moves across the ice and snow. Each toe has a thick, curved, non-retractable claw which is used for traction when running or climbing on ice or for grasping the bear's kill and making it incapable of escape. The soles of the feet have small bumps and cavities that act like suction cups and help keep them from slipping. The eyes, whose vision is at least as good as in

Polar bears have been around for about one hundred thousand years and are the top predator in the Arctic.

humans, are dark brown, set fairly close together and looking forward, as you might expect in a creature that is more often hunter than hunted.

As warm-blooded mammals, polar bears can regulate their body heat at a fairly steady temperature. By having a thick layer of blubber under the skin they can stay warm even in the coldest environment. In strong sunlight, meanwhile, the bear's black skin helps soak up as much heat as possible. Each year the bears will moult completely, usually in May or June, shedding and replacing their coat in a process that can last several weeks. The only parts of the animal not covered in fur are the nose and the pads on the feet, which are also black.

Their compact body shape also helps insulate them in bitter weather. Since large objects lose heat slowly, it's the heaviest polar bears that stay warm for the longest time. In addition to their layer of blubber, even when air temperatures drop below minus 40 degrees their body heat is maintained by their thick fur and very tough hide. At times indeed they can be almost too well insulated during the summer months, and if they have to move fast they do tend to overheat. To compensate for this, unless on the attack they move slowly in the main and rest a lot. In summer,

Even when yawning a polar bear presents a fearsome aspect. Note the size of the paw…

when in any case the shrinkage of the sea ice can make hunting difficult, polar bears can conserve energy by remaining inactive for over 80 per cent of the time. On warm days or after physical activity, they will sprawl out on the ground or the surface of the ice, often on their backs with their feet in the air. Or, like a human, they can swim to cool down.

Understandably perhaps, because they are so well built for insulation against the cold, polar bears give off no detectable heat. One effect of this is that they never show up in infrared photography, designed to measure warmth. For example, one scientist's attempt to photograph a polar bear with infrared film produced nothing more than a print with one single spot on it. This image simply represented the puff of air caused by the bear's breath.

When they're not hunting, polar bears often conserve energy by sleeping or resting. They tend to be at their most lively for the first third of the day. By the final third they are at their least active – something I can identify with after years of doing the Capital Radio Breakfast Show. If need be, a polar bear will nap just about anywhere and at any time. In the winter months, to save body heat they'll sleep in pits that they've dug out in the snow, trying to position themselves so that they will have their side or their back to the wind. In blizzard conditions they will sleep for several days curled up like this until the storm passes, to wake up covered with a thick blanket of snow.

Apart from hunting and competing bloodily for a mate, sometimes polar bears also take part in violent play-fighting. To an outsider this can look terrifying, but in fact it's no more vicious than the same kind of contest between most other creatures in the animal kingdom. What makes these fights so awe-inspiring is that the bears, hissing and growling, are so loud and so huge. The point of these clashes is a reaction to each other's presence that simply involves testing each other. When polar bears do fight for real, it's horrifically obvious that each is out to kill his adversary. Play-fighting is very different. A male bear usually initiates the encounter by approaching another male with his head down, mouth closed and eyes looking away. The bears make contact by touching or mouthing each other around the face and neck. They then rear up on their hind legs and try to push each other over with their forepaws.

Even in their movements, polar bears are conditioned by their adaptation to the Arctic cold. When walking or running they expend more than

Above left: Bears conserve energy by remaining inactive for 80 per cent of the time.

Below left: Males fighting. They play fight to test each other but they also fight, sometimes to the death, over mates.

twice the energy used by most other animals. This is largely due to their enormous physical bulk. Although they are able to gallop for a short distance as fast as any horse, polar bears will always prefer a leisurely amble to a brisk pace. Their walk is distinctive, in the form of a steady lumbering gait. The front paws swing outwards with each step, landing slightly pigeon toed, and the head moves gently from side to side.

Like humans, polar bears walk on the soles of their feet, their heels touching the ground first. Like other bears, they can stand on their hind feet, and walk upright for a few paces at a time. If you are unlucky enough to find yourself in the path of such an animal, almost no sight on earth is ever likely to be more frightening.

Their very existence has been threatened, by humans who've hunted them not just for need but for sport.

Throughout the habitat of the polar bear's world population, the ocean temperatures average about one degree Celsius. However, the fear for the future, ultimately affecting much of the planet, is that, with global warming, each year the amount of polar ice is growing less. In the dozens of millennia since polar bears evolved to their present form they have been perfectly adapted to thrive in harsh places. During more recent times, however, their very existence has been threatened by humans who've hunted them not just from need but for sport. Until laws were passed – just in time – to protect the bears from being hunted, parts of the Arctic resembled a slaughterhouse. More recently, climate change threatens the polar bear, mainly through a large-scale loss of habitat. Pollution too is a danger to the bears' well-being, standing as they do at the top of a food chain. The best hope for these extraordinary creatures is that mankind, having drawn back once from their destruction, can still find ways to help them survive.

Bears prefer to live and hunt on sea ice – close to their food supplies.

Introduction

I have always loved bears …

I've always been fascinated by bears. I've also found them utterly terrifying. The Inuits have a word for the emotions evoked by a polar bear – 'ilyra'. It means 'fear mixed with awe'. A friend who ran a safari park once told me that the animal he feared the most would always be the bear. Even the most aggressive big cat, he said, would usually show its intentions towards you. But a bear would attack with no warning. For four days a week they would happily let you feed them, and on the fifth day they'd turn and kill you.

Over the years, before I'd ever caught sight of a polar bear, I'd seen many other bears – brown and black in Russia and Canada, and enormous grizzlies in Alaska. The first one of all was in Alaska. It happened in the middle of the night and the bear was running like hell, in a panic.

I was on a fishing trip to the beautiful Chosen River. We had been warned that there were a lot of grizzly bears in the area. But we'd also been told that, so long as we were careful, and stayed close to our guide, they shouldn't be a problem.

However, at the end of our first day, it became evident that there actually was a problem – a serious one. What was judged by its footprints to be a very large grizzly had been visiting our camp regularly during the small hours of the morning. Although wary of humans, it had found the smell of cooking too good to ignore. So much so that the amiable American family who ran the camp, the Duncans, were worried that sooner or later there would be a confrontation between a bear and one of the guests.

At this point Bobby Duncan, the youngest and easily the maddest of the family, decided to set his own version of a bear trap. It was one of the most splendid and absurd creations I have ever seen. That night, he settled himself to sleep on the cookhouse floor, with a loaded shotgun by his side. A rope was tied to his big toe, and fastened at the other end to a large steel table. This was just outside the cook tent and covered in fresh salmon, with a couple of pounds of sausages. Saucepan lids, metal trays and tin cans were also scattered across the table top.

Fresh paw prints in the snow. Don't follow them.

At breakfast next morning, Bobby was still fast asleep on the floor, with the rope attached firmly as ever to his big toe. Next night too there was no Mr Bear. By the third night we'd almost forgotten that Bobby was tucked up again on the cookhouse floor with his trap at the ready.

About two o'clock next morning, however, an enormous crash was followed by a terrifying roar, and two booming blasts from a gun. We emerged from our tents to see flashlamps everywhere and not one bear but two, racing away from the camp at a speed that wouldn't have disgraced a cheetah. Bobby Duncan was grinning in triumph. He had blasted both barrels over the heads of the bears, who were unlikely to come to the camp again. In fact no bears came round to it for the rest of that summer.

Alaska was also the first place where I became aware of the disturbing sensation that people mean by 'feeling the bears'. This expression is used to describe sensing the presence of bears, but without actually seeing them. I have since experienced it many, many times.

Even the most aggressive big cat would usually show its intentions towards you. But a bear would attack with no warning. For four days they would happily let you feed them, and on the fifth day they'd turn and kill you.

Too close for comfort, a bear begins to show signs of interest in the photographer.

We were salmon fishing, and our guide had dropped us by the Chosen River where it reaches the top of a long gravel run. The routine was for him to sit in the boat, supposedly on red alert, while we fished downriver for an hour or so. I say 'supposedly' because I'm convinced that a lot of the time my armed-to-the-teeth-ever-vigilant guide was actually catching up on a bit of sleep.

On several occasions, walking back through thick forest in which the biggest grizzly could easily hide, I'd discovered huge paw prints somewhere along the very path I had taken about an hour before. But each time, our guide insisted that he hadn't been asleep and that these were old paw prints from many days ago.

Well, they looked pretty damn fresh to me. Some overlapped the boot marks I'd left that day when going the other way. The final giveaway came one morning when, returning to the boat and 'Hawkeye', my guide, I passed an enormous pile of fresh, steaming bear dung. The guide did sheepishly admit that he might have closed his eyes for just a few minutes.

This was the evidence left by big grizzly bears that presumably had come out, taken a quick look, and decided not to eat me that particular morning.

Most bears do this, most of the time. There are many accounts of grizzly bear attacks, but not many records of fatalities. After making an initial terrifying charge, usually the bear will back off. But compared to other members of the bear family, the polar bear is much more aggressive, and one of the few animals that will sometimes follow the scent of a human in order to hunt him down. Like most animals the polar bear would usually rather back away from man – but not always. He is the ultimate dangerous predator. If he attacks he will usually kill, and if he kills he will probably eat his prey.

He is the ultimate dangerous predator. If he attacks he will usually kill, and if he kills he will probably eat his prey.

Showing its teeth, growling and shaking – sure signs of aggressive intent.

Only a very small and exclusive club exists of people who have survived a polar bear attack. Currently its membership worldwide is believed to number less than ten.

But, though terrifying, polar bears are also beautiful, graceful and hugely impressive. Since first seeing pictures of them as a little boy in my 'Big Book of Bears' I had also wanted to see one in the wild. As I started to encounter other kinds of bear on fishing trips in the years that followed, the obsession had grown. More than anything I wanted to get close – but not too close – to a polar bear.

It had become one of those things you have to do before you die. So, last summer, with a bit of free time in my life for once, I set out on what proved to be one of the most enthralling journeys of my life.

Longyearbyen

As our starting point in the Arctic we had decided to fly up to Longyearbyen, capital of the Svalbard group of islands in the extreme north of Norway. It is also the most northerly commercial airport on earth, 700 miles or so north of Oslo, and only about 400 miles south of the Pole.

The Svalbard archipelago is the size of Ireland, and two-thirds of it are permanently covered with ice and snow. It's difficult to imagine this place as it was 300 million years ago, but at that time Svalbard was in the tropics. Continental drift shifted it to its present sub-polar location, and most of its landscape was created during the ice ages of the last two million years. Here the dark polar night lasts from October to the end of February, during which time temperatures drop to 30 or 40 degrees below freezing. We were visiting, however, during the months of the midnight sun, from April through to August which, with twenty-four hours a day of dazzling non-stop sunlight, were a cameraman's dream.

Above: Crosses mark the graves of miners killed in coalmine accidents in Longyearbyen.

Right: Flying in to Longyearbyen.

Next page: Four hundred miles south of the North Pole...

Longyearbyen began its existence as the main point of export for coal from the rich seams laid down during the islands' early tropical pre-history. Crosses standing on the hill that looks down on the little town are a tragic testimony to the fatal accidents suffered over the years by local miners. Mostly, however, life here is geared to an awareness of the polar bears, who are never far away. In the airport is a sign reminding visitors that, 'You are a guest in the kingdom of the polar bear.' Everywhere there is evidence of the dangers posed by living at close quarters to the bears. The most recent edition of the local paper, the *Svalbard News*, carried a terrifying picture on its front page of an incident that had happened only a few days before. A remote seafront cottage a mile or so outside the centre of Longyearbyen had been attacked by a polar bear. An intrepid if foolhardy cameraman had actually managed to get a shot of the animal

Life here is geared to an awareness of polar bears, who are never far away. In the airport is a sign: 'You are in the kingdom of the polar bear'.

smashing through the door. The bear, who was hunting for food, stood almost as tall as the house, and created enormous damage. Fortunately, since they were away shopping in town, the owners of the property had a lucky escape.

In order to set out on our adventure by sea from Longyearbyen, back in London we had made arrangements through an extraordinarily helpful company called Norwegian Coastal Voyage. Through them we were to travel the area in a small cruise ship, the *Polar Star*. She was a converted ice-breaker, not particularly large but very comfortable. As well as her crew, and James, a helpful young guy from NCV, there was a number of passengers besides us. They included one or two other hardy explorers, plus a few scientists. In our own party, including my wife Ingrid and me, there were seven of us. Martin Founds and his wife Jean run a travel company

As we went on board to load cameras, sound equipment and boxes of film we were all full of excitement.

Fellow bear enthusiasts on the *Polar Star* (next page) go through their survival drills.

called Martin's World. Martin is also a brilliant photographer with whom I've travelled all over Canada. Our film crew of three was made up of Geraint on camera, Richard the soundman, who I'd worked with before in the rather warmer climate of Tanzania, and Dave, our director, a good mate of mine who I'd last met in Peru.

We were to cruise to the very north of the islands, way above the 80-degree parallel. One of the ship's crew looked positively gleeful as he promised how the weather would become much colder, amid more and more ice. As the ice increased, however, so would our chances of spotting and filming any polar bears. To get from the mother ship onto the shore we would be able to use a small Zodiac inflatable boat with an outboard motor. We also had an armed guide called Erik, and with luck we might even get at least a few hours' use of a rescue helicopter for filming from the air. An organization called North Face had kindly provided a mountain of protective clothing, and as we went on board to load cameras, sound equipment and boxes of film we were all full of excitement.

The hunt was on ...

We were to cruise to the very north of the islands. As the ice increased, so did our chances of spotting polar bears.

The Gun Shop

In Longyearbyen there are warning signs everywhere with bears on them, and you get a sense all the time that the bears are watching from the hills which form a perfect circle above the town. You can imagine them licking their lips as each planeload of visitors arrives, perhaps seeing it as a possible meals on wheels service. Whether or not you can see him, the polar bear is never far away. There are over 2,500 bears in the Svalbard area, and they are to be treated with much respect.

On arrival, therefore, I was told that one essential is a gun. When I pointed out to the nice man in the tourist office that I hadn't actually packed a rifle capable of bringing down a polar bear, he said, 'No problem. You can hire one from the shop.' Now, apart from a few hours trying to hit clay pigeons, I've never fired a gun and I've certainly never owned one. But all the same, off we went to the gun shop.

Puzzlingly, it was run by a Geordie, called Edwin. What his story was we were too polite to ask, but he'd lived in this remote spot in northern Norway for many years. During this time he hadn't been back home, nor, apparently, would he ever return. Possibly he's a book in himself. What was plain to see was that he ran a hugely well-stocked gun shop, which was clearly thriving as a business. He very patiently found us just the guns we'd need and showed us how to use them. But, and this is the weird thing, nobody asked us for a passport or even a current utility bill, let alone a shotgun licence. For the princely sum of 100 kroner – less than ten quid – per day, both my cameraman and I were fitted out with guns, plus live ammunition, that from a couple of miles away could blow a hole in a rhinoceros. Alternatively, for ninety quid we could have bought a gun outright.

Edwin then told us in detail the drill to follow if you find yourself close up to a hungry bear.

Above: Rifles are used only as a last resort but a polar bear is an extraordinarily dangerous animal and since there are 2,500 of them in the immediate vicinity everyone in Svalbard carries a gun.

Right: For just £9 per day you too can be Wyatt Earp.

Polar bears don't usually look on humans as food, but a really famished bear will eat almost anything. Young animals are often the most dangerous, because they've gained only limited hunting skills and may have a hard time catching anything to eat. Animals weakened by age or by injuries have a similar problem and they too can be extremely threatening. The same kind of hazard is often caused by surprising a bear, as it may well feel it has to defend itself. Most dangerous of all are probably females, or sows, with cubs, who will fight to the death – almost certainly yours – to protect their young.

Only use the rifle as a last resort. Repeated rifle shots or flares, so we were advised, will nearly always make the bear back off. I have to say I didn't much like Edwin's use of 'nearly'.

If a polar bear does move directly towards you, it's recommended that you make as much noise as possible – by shouting and clapping your hands, or by starting up the engine if you're on a snowmobile or in a boat. Usually this is enough to make the bear withdraw. However, if the bear contines to advance towards you or your campsite, the suggestion is always to use a flare gun as a first option – this was something else that Edwin told us to carry – and only use the rifle as a last resort. If you do fire a flare, try and land it between you and the bear. Having the flare fall behind the bear may only make it come towards you even faster. If you use a rifle to frighten the animal away, try not to shoot into the ground too close to it, as it may be hurt by a ricochet. Repeated rifle shots or flares, so we were advised, will nearly always make the bear back off. I have to say I didn't much like Edwin's use of 'nearly'.

In fact I found all his advice terrifying. If a bear continues to attack, with no sign of being frightened away by warning shots, as a last resort you must shoot to kill. Bearing in mind that you must probably make any decision within a matter of a few seconds, it may help to know in advance that you should aim only for the chest. Do not attempt a shot in the head, because the skull of a polar bear is very tough, and protected by heavy muscle. The vulnerable area in the chest is surprisingly small for such an enormous animal. Keep shooting until the bear lies still, and don't approach it until you are sure it is dead.

Above: Ready for anything I take up a defensive position. Luckily the gun is not loaded.

Next page: With the film crew Geraint, Richard and Dave. I don't think the sign says 'Bears Crossing'.

The final instruction is not to move the bear nor remove anything from the scene, and to contact the office of the local Syssel-mann, or Governor, immediately. Any bear that has to be killed must nonetheless be accounted for in minute detail, and fines for shooting any polar bear unnecessarily, particularly if an attack from one is found to be your fault, are massive.

Although this information is vital for everyone travelling in polar bear country, it is probable that you will never need to use it. Guns are nevertheless very much a part of life on Svalbard. The local Governor later told us that on average in every household in Longyearbyen there are about three guns. In itself this is hard to believe in such an anxious age. Since no nation is arguably more worried than America about security, what followed next day was even more extraordinary. We were filming some general views around the airfield when Hilary Clinton, former First Lady, US Senator, and possibly the next President, flew in on some environmental mission. Although Senator Clinton was surrounded by the usual security men running everywhere like headless chickens, they walked straight past my cameraman and me, both of us armed to the teeth with our hire 'em by the day shotguns.

Had Hilary's security people really done their homework? On the other hand, despite the number of guns in every house throughout Longyearbyen, it has to be said that in the case of this little town the crime rate is virtually nil.

Barentsburg

There's a bear's heart in the museum at Barentsburg. Apparently it was a gift to the Governor many years ago, although whether the Governor was particularly pleased to receive it or not, has never been recorded. It's certainly impressive in a revolting sort of way – very large, bright red and preserved in formaldehyde. There is also, in the same museum, a quite massive polar bear in front of which easily pleased visitors like myself can't resist being photographed. It is absolutely enormous and made me feel tiny.

We found the town one of the most depressing places on earth. It's drab, the conditions are appalling and temperatures can drop as far as minus 40 degrees. But the polar bears are a constant presence.

Barentsburg itself is the first stop out of Longyearbyen, as you head north towards the 80-degree parallel and the thickest of the ice. This tough mining town has the extraordinary feel of a time warp. It's actually part of Norway but everything about it is Russian and old Soviet Russian at that. The drab houses, built in the shadow of the coalmines, carry old Soviet union insignia, and flags from the days of the USSR. The letters CCCP are everywhere as a souvenir of the era of Kruschev, Bulganin and Brezhnev, and there are still giant images of Stalin. Coal has been mined in Barentsburg since around the year 1900, as one of the main sources for the old mining company of Kulkompaniet Isefjord Spitsbergen. The mines are still actively working, shipping coal to Murmansk and Archangel, but like everything else in town their equipment has seen better days. Much of it is obsolete and constantly breaking down. Here too there have been a number of mining accidents, several of them fatal. The town itself was more or less destroyed by the German Navy towards the end of the Second World War and has never been properly rebuilt.

Being savaged by a stuffed bear in the museum at Barentsburg.

There is one hotel, called, unadventurously, the Barentsburg Hotel, where we bravely risked a meal of Russian boiled pork and potatoes with Arctic sorrel and cabbage. To be honest it was only about as good as it sounds but the accompanying vodka, provided in half-pint mugs, was very welcome and so potent it would have brought down a walrus.

I have to say that, arriving at Barentsburg, we found the town one of the most depressing places on earth, and yet there was a real fascination in visiting this anachronistic settlement. Everything about the place belongs to an age gone by and probably not a very nice age. But bizarrely the Russians who come there to work, mainly from regions like the Ukraine and Siberia, do everything they can to stay.

Virtually every worker in the town is employed by the mines, as there is nothing else to provide any sort of income. The normal deal for the workers who come in from Russia is a two-year contract. But at the end of that time most try to stay on for at least another year or so by renewing their contract in any devious way they can. Some of them have been there for twenty years. The place is drab, the conditions in the mines are appalling and in winter the temperature drops as far as minus 40. Yet the Russians there told me about it being 'a fine place to live' and how they all loved the 'mild climate' – so however dull can it be and however cold does it get back home in Siberia?

As in Longyearbyen the polar bears are a constant presence. Just five days before our arrival a large male bear, or boar, had been spotted in the early morning on the outskirts of Barentsburg. Mercifully any confrontation was avoided when at daybreak it moved away as the first buses started to run carrying workers to the mines. It must have been an incongruous sight as it strolled past the neighbourhood's giant pictures of Stalin.

Above: Arriving at Barentsburg.

Right :The mining town of Barentsburg, where the temperature drops as far as minus 40.

Next page: An eerily beautiful seascape.

Ny-Ålesund

Left: The most northerly post office on the planet. Don't expect next day delivery.

Next page: The bare mist-shrouded mountains of Svalbard.

Perhaps the strangest and most unearthly sound we heard throughout our trip was when the *Polar Star* sailed into the harbour at Ny-Ålesund. At first we were too bewildered to work out what it was. Eventually we realized that what we heard was the welcome from a hastily assembled brass band.

Ny-Ålesund is peopled almost entirely by scientists, and whatever they do in their spare time, it's clearly not band practice. To this day I couldn't swear what the tune was, though the consensus of opinion holds that it might have been 'When The Saints Come Marching In'. But we smiled respectfully at what was in any case a nice gesture and shook hands with everybody in sight before we went to explore this extraordinary little town.

It was originally a small mining community, although today scientific research has taken it over almost entirely. A perfect ring of glaciers surrounds the town, providing an awesome backdrop. Sited on the latitude of 79 degrees north it is part of the high Arctic, a region of permafrost. In Ny-Ålesund this means that even during the summer months, the topsoil only thaws to a depth of 4–20 inches. In winter, from about 20 October to 20 February, the sun never rises above the horizon. During the darkest period, around Christmas, there is literally no difference between night and day. The wildlife includes reindeer, ptarmigan and a regular population of polar bears.

The town square proudly boasts what is almost certainly the most northerly post office on earth. Since by any standards the postal service can be bad enough at home, we decided not to test how long it would take a letter to get there even with a first-class stamp.

The other thing that dominates the square in the middle of this hamlet-sized town is a massive bust of Roald Amundsen. Ny-Ålesund was very much the centre of this extraordinary man's exploration of the north polar regions. During the course of a breathtaking career, Amundsen's original goal was to travel the North-West Passage. To that end, in 1905 in his ship *Gjoa* he and his crew set off from Norway. Eventually they became trapped in the ice. Undeterred, they continued by dog-sled,

A perfect ring of glaciers surrounds the town, providing an awesome backdrop. In winter the sun never rises above the horizon. During the darkest period there is literally no difference between night and day.

to arrive over 540 miles away at a place called Eagle Alaska as the first men ever to traverse the North-West Passage.

Amundsen's next goal was the North Pole. But while he was still busy with setting up the expedition, in 1909 news came that the American explorer Robert Peary had beaten him to it. Amundsen switched his attention instead to the South Pole. This meant trying to overtake the British expedition led by Captain Robert Scott, who had already set out for Antarctica from New Zealand. When Scott and his depleted team arrived at the Pole, on 17 January 1912, to his horror he found Amundsen's Norwegian flag already planted there.

These achievements would last most men a lifetime, but the Ny-Ålesund air seems to harden the resolve. On 11 May 1926, Amundsen, sponsored by a great friend, the American Lincoln Ellsworth, set out to fly from Svalbard to Alaska. He and his crew crash landed, short of the Pole, and were eventually rescued at sea in bitter conditions. Amundsen was not one to be put off, and next year he tried again. With Ellsworth and the Italian explorer Umberto Nobile, he crossed the North Pole sixteen hours after they'd left Spitsbergen, dropping the Norwegian, American and Italian flags right on the site. Three days later, having covered 3,274 miles in seventy-two hours, they made a triumphant landing in Alaska, having become the first men to have flown from Europe to America over the top of the world. They were able to confirm that there was no land in the area of the North Pole. Thus the last blank on the world map was filled in. Considering the extraordinarily harsh conditions in that part of the world, and the fact that huge developments in polar clothing, food and navigational techniques had not yet been achieved, Amundsen and his fellow explorers stand out as truly heroic figures.

But in May 1928 tragedy followed the news that Umberto Nobile's new airship, the *Italia*, had crashed somewhere in the high Arctic latitudes. Without hesitation Amundsen volunteered to attempt a rescue and flew out with five other men from the north coast of Norway. Ironically, Nobile and his crew were to be rescued days later. But three hours after takeoff, Amundsen's plane transmitted what were to be its final signals. The aircraft never returned.

The massive bust of Roald Amundsen, which dominates the square in Ny-Ålesund.

The air in Ny-Ålesund seems to harden the resolve. Having covered 3,390 miles in seventy-two hours, Amundsen and Nobile made a triumphant landing in Alaska, having become the first men to have flown from Europe to America over the top of the world.

The Most Northerly Man
on the Planet

It's generally agreed that the northern limit of the world's polar bear population is around the 80-degree latitude. Very rarely, individual bears have been tracked venturing almost up to the North Pole. But above 80 degrees it's barren and bitterly cold, with little other life for the bears to feed on.

It's also about as far north as most ships can safely travel, even in summer.

The morning we were due to cross the 80-degree mark our Captain and crew were clearly excited – it was obviously a great moment for all of them, particularly since in some seasons it's not possible to voyage this far. There was a real buzz on board, and everybody had come on deck, peering through the grey light to the north of us as if expecting to see something.

When we actually crossed the magic parallel the atmosphere became quite emotional. The ship's engines slowed, and the Captain sounded a bell and made what was probably a very moving speech. Unfortunately, as it was in Norwegian almost none of us understood a word, but we seemed to say 'Skol' in all the right places, and at the end we clapped loudly. Everybody then shook hands with everyone else on board and the ship's crew brought round glasses of champagne with the Captain's compliments. It was a fine moment.

I did manage to convince a rather credulous American woman that somewhere out there in the ocean there was a sign marking 80 degrees but that the freezing mist all around us was making it difficult to see. When we left her to go back to our cabins I swear she was still looking for the sign.

Next morning we cruised even further north, to the limit of how far we could go towards the Pole. There was still land close by, but at 82 degrees we had come right to the edge of the thick ice that stretched unbroken all the way to the North Pole. Even in summer it was bitterly cold, and there was freezing fog all around us. It was an altogether eerie place.

The *Polar Star*, a former icebreaker, forges a passage through the ice.

Then the Captain told us an extraordinary thing. If we took our Zodiac and went ashore at this point, we could film in the sure knowledge that we were the most northerly people on the planet. It really captured our imagination to hear that although there was a scientific research station in the area, and a trapper or two, they were all several miles to the south of us.

Leaving the mother ship, we carefully made our way through the surrounding icebergs in our little cramped rubber dinghy, mindful of the risks from capsizing in this freezing sea. As we got out of our Zodiac and scrunched our way up through the snow we felt immensely privileged. We set up an amazing shot with huge glaciers all around and, behind me to the south as I stood in the foreground, the ship, clearly visible from half a mile away.

Left: The sea ice at 82 degrees latitude becomes too thick to go further.

Above and next page: 'At this moment I am the most northerly man on the planet...'

I was just about to utter the immortal words, 'I am the most northerly man on the planet' when Dave, our director, said, 'Hang on, what about him?' At that point we all realized, as would any television viewer with half a brain cell, that, to get the shot with the ship in the background, our cameraman Geraint would have to be somewhere between me and the Pole, i.e. further north.

Doh!

It just wouldn't have the same impact to have me claiming excitedly that I was the planet's second most northerly man. After a hasty conference we abandoned the jolly wheeze of having the *Polar Star* in the background, turned the camera right round, with me this time in front of a massive wall of ice. Only then could I, with conviction, announce that 'at this moment I am the most northerly man on the planet ...There are six point four billion people on earth and at this moment every single one of them is south of me!'

We all took it in turns to stand and be photographed in 'the spot' and then made our triumphant way back to the *Polar Star* and its nice warm bar. It had been a great day.

We had come right to the edge of the thick ice that stretched unbroken all the way to the North Pole. Even in summer it was bitterly cold, and there was freezing fog all around us. It was an eerie place.

Stalking the Caribou

Of all the wildlife in the Arctic, photographing the caribou can be particularly difficult. This beautiful, agile creature is, like most other members of the deer family, extremely shy. My friend Martin and I had once spotted a large herd when up in the extreme north of Canada near Hudson's Bay, and spent most of a frustrating afternoon trying to get close enough for some decent photographs. But every time they got even a hint of our scent they moved away. They never panicked or bolted, but they always kept us at a distance of about 100 yards, so that even with our longest lenses we couldn't get a decent close-up.

It was all the more exciting when, driving home towards Longyearbyen one evening, Martin and I saw a lone caribou quietly grazing a couple of miles outside the town. We thought that if we were careful we just might get close enough for a reasonably good photograph of the animal, with me in the foreground.

> This beautiful, agile creature is, like most other members of the deer family, extremely shy. We thought that if we were careful we might get close enough for a reasonably good photograph, with me in the foreground.

We very quietly switched off the engine of our four-wheel drive and closed its doors as gently as we could. Martin got out his camera and a range of lenses. We were only about 200 yards away but the animal seemed to take little notice.

Stalking the lone caribou. At this stage it was about 200 yards away. Stealth was essential.

Talking in whispers, to avoid the caribou panicking at our scent we moved round to where the wind blew into our faces. Slowly we crept towards the still-munching animal. We'd got within 100 yards when the caribou moved sharply and looked straight at me. 'Get ready, Martin,' I said. 'It's gonna bolt.' For a few agonizing seconds we stood, not daring to breathe. Then not only did it not bolt, but it went back to chewing the Arctic grass.

Even more carefully now, certain that we were pushing our luck, we tried to get just a bit closer. I was now within 20 yards of the creature, hardly daring to look up. Again it lifted its magnificent antlered head and seemed to stare straight at me. Martin and I froze on the spot. After what seemed like an age, the caribou put its head back down and carried on feeding.

One more time we tiptoed forward, but by now we knew absolutely that at any second the animal would spook off at high speed. The need for

Unbelievably, the caribou stood still enough for me to reach out and stroke him. Our skilful stalking had been little short of magnificent... but our joy was rather spoiled the next morning.

Our stalking allowed us to get close enough to take this shot of the caribou.

silence and speed was agonizing as I edged even closer. Each click of Martin's shutter sounded like a gunshot. But Martin, grinning with satisfaction, whispered to me that we'd already got some fantastic pictures.

I got as close as five yards ... three ... two ... one ... and then, unbelievably, the caribou stood still enough for me to reach out and stroke him. Our skilful stalking had been little short of magnificent. All the way home we congratulated ourselves, and could hardly wait to tell everybody over dinner. Not only were we heroes, but the joy of having a digital camera also meant that we could view some of the splendid close-ups of our caribou that same evening.

Our joy was rather spoiled next morning. Walking through the main street of Longyearbyen we came across the same caribou. Apparently for several years it had been the town's pet. Which is why, the second time it was sighted by us, it was giving the local children a ride.

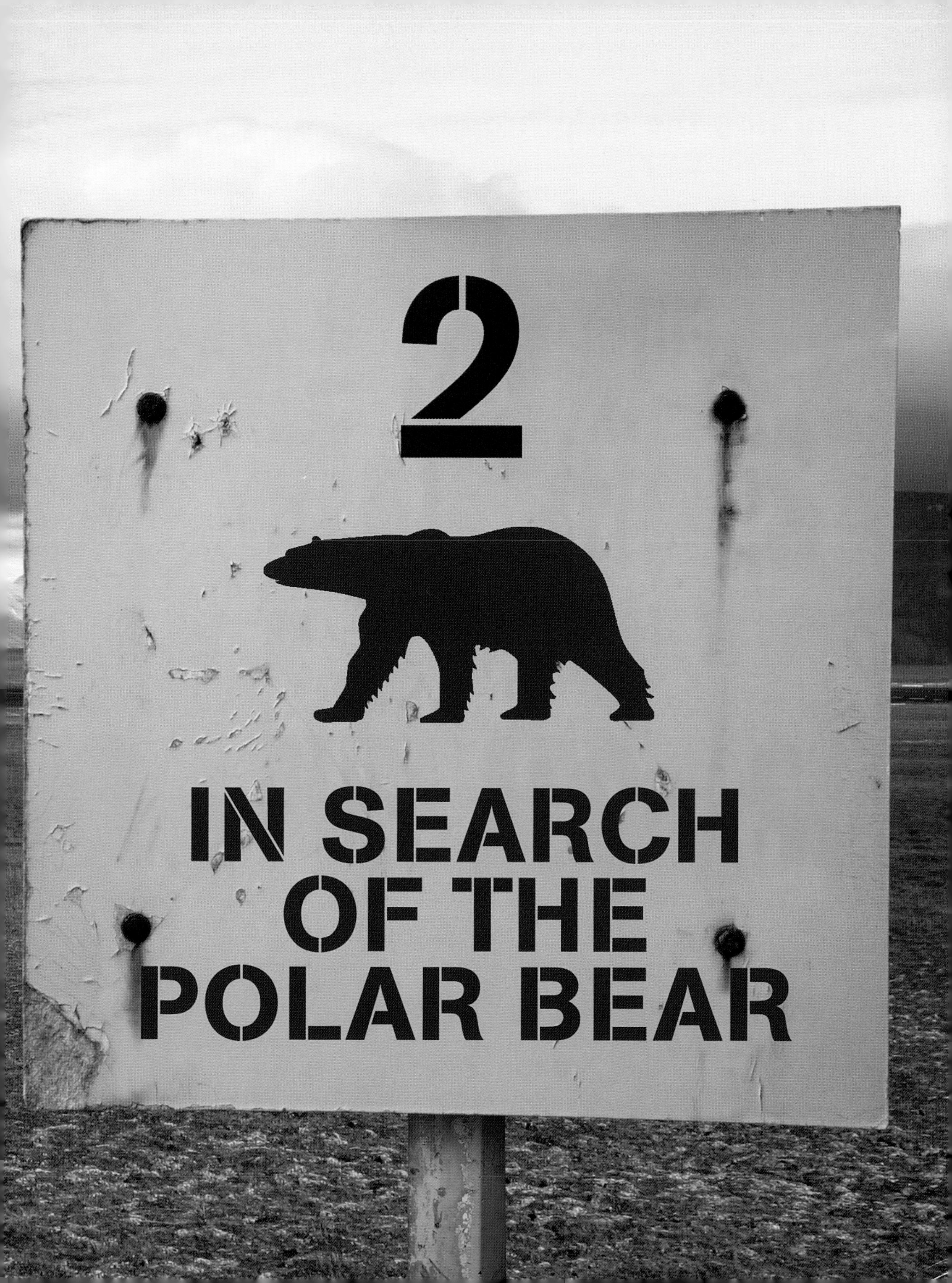
2
IN SEARCH
OF THE
POLAR BEAR

Turning the Ship Around

This was going to be hugely embarrassing.

'Oh, no. He's turning round,' muttered James.

'Not now,' I said. 'It won't still be there. It's been nearly an hour.'

But there was no mistake. Again the Captain's voice rang out over the Tannoy. Slowly the *Polar Star* was going into its huge turning circle and heading back to where we'd just been. The bad thing about this was knowing it was all down to 'the English'. Specifically … me.

After a splendid dinner with a couple of glasses of wine, we'd settled into what had become a pleasant evening ritual, sitting up on deck, drink in hand, peering through our cameras and binoculars. We usually sat up chatting and filming till well into the small hours, as in any case it was always broad daylight.

**Above and right:
The ship turns around
because I *think* I have
seen a bear.**

**Next page: I was right.
Cameras at the ready…**

Each evening, cruising just off-shore into the midnight sun, we were constantly on the lookout for wildlife. In particular of course we hoped for a sighting of polar bears. Tonight we'd already passed a group of beluga whales. As our luxury icebreaker approached, they hadn't panicked at all, just moved a bit further out to sea in order to put more distance between them and us.

We'd seen Arctic foxes everywhere, and kittiwakes and black-backed gulls had followed us all the time, silently hanging 30 feet or so above the wake of our ship. But as we cruised for hour after hour searching the shoreline with our binoculars, there was still no sign of any bear.

With an estimated 2,500 polar bears on Svalbard, it was amazing that you could travel a whole day without spotting even one. But it happens.

The fjord where we found ourselves that night made the search for wildlife hard in any case. We had to keep the statutory 100 yards off-shore, the sun was streaming into our eyes even though it was one o'clock in

We were constantly on the lookout for wildlife – especially bears. With two and a half thousand polar bears on Svalbard, it's amazing that you can travel a whole day without spotting even one. But it happens.

the morning and, although there was no snow at this point, the cliffs were covered in thick grasses, heather and gorse. Above all, the ground was littered with white rocks, deposited there over thousands of years by passing glaciers.

Each of these white rocks looked like a polar bear, and there had already been several false alarms. One Danish scientist was convinced his rock was a polar bear until two mountain hares climbed on top of it to watch us go by. One of the crew tactfully pointed out that unless they wanted to be dinner in about five seconds, hares were unlikely to risk standing on the head of a polar bear.

But then, as I swung my binoculars for the umpteenth time along the view of the shoreline rocks, I saw a pair of ears! Not huge, but unmistakably ears, and white ones at that. Then, just as suddenly, they were gone.

'I've just seen a bear – just over there – that white rock is a bear!' I said, almost shaking. I was absolutely certain.

'I've just seen a bear,' I said – 'just over there – that white rock is a bear.' It didn't help my credibility that there were literally thousands of white rocks immediately in front of us. But at that moment I was absolutely certain. I ran excitedly to the ship's crew. 'Bear!' I said, almost shaking – 'Just over there – that white rock is a bear.'

'Whereabouts?' they asked.

'Just there,' I replied. By now, however, even I couldn't be sure of precisely where it had been. I was pointing at what seemed no more than a maze of white rocks.

'How big was it?' I was asked.

'Was it a male or a female?'

'Well, I'm not really sure … er …I only saw some ears.'

Perhaps understandably, the Norwegians were less than impressed. After training their binoculars along the rocks and scrutinizing them for a few minutes with their much more expert eyes, they slowly went back to whatever they had been doing. The ship rumbled relentlessly on.

'Don't worry,' said the Captain. 'This happens every night.'

'I'm still sure I saw a bear,' I mumbled, feeling rather less confident.

He said, 'There's a big bay coming up in about ten minutes. We usually see bears around there.' We cruised on, with me feeling humbled by the whole incident.

As we came around into Bear Bay the skipper cut the engines. We all got our cameras on standby and everybody came on deck. This stretch of coastline really did seem like bear country. There were worried-looking seals bunched up at the water's edge, and at any second we expected to see bears stalking them. Again, there was that sense of being watched.

But after twenty minutes of straining to examine every inch of Bear Bay, by degrees we realized that this evening Mr Bear wasn't there after all, or at least he wasn't in the mood to be photographed. Among all of us there was a sense of disappointment. After the miles we'd covered today, perhaps we really were fated to crawl into our beds without sighting a single bear. Even the Captain looked a bit dejected.

Then he turned to me and asked, 'Are you sure you saw a bear?'

'Well, I was at the time. But there are so many white rocks, and in any case it was only a pair of ears really…' I heard my voice trail off feebly.

But the Captain had already disappeared, being, I thought, even more bored with my ramblings than I was. Suddenly, though, his voice came over the ship's Tannoy system. 'Bear sighting,' it said – 'Bear sighting. The English have seen a polar bear. I repeat, the English have seen a polar bear back along the shore. We are now turning the ship and going back to see it.'

This was going to be truly embarrassing.

I was mortified. No longer was I confident that there'd been a bear in the first place. Maybe there hadn't even been a pair of ears. Or, if there had been, perhaps they belonged to a fox, or a mountain hare. After all, the ears on a mountain hare are enormous, and they are white. Maybe all I'd seen was a couple of ear-shaped rocks, or some ear-shaped Arctic plant. My confidence was nil.

All sort of unwelcome thoughts ran through my mind as we cruised back to the scene of the 'English sighting'. This had happened over an hour ago, so surely the bear, if indeed there had ever been a bear, would now be long gone.

As we approached the area again, I despaired. Even though it had been an honest mistake I knew I'd get funny looks from the Captain and his

crew for the rest of the voyage. If after this I was foolish enough to think I'd spotted anything, even an Arctic worm, I'd keep it to myself. The strange thing was that my own crew were as embarrassed as I was. They weren't at all ready to catch my eye, but looked down at their boots as if all of them were somehow sharing in the shame of the English – even our cameraman, who came from Wales.

What came next over the Tannoy was music – to my ears at least. It was the voice of the Captain.

'Polar bear on the shoreline. Polar bear on the shoreline Thank you to the English!' Under his voice, on the Tannoy there could be heard the unmistakable sound of grateful applause. Up on deck, the ship's company and crew hurried towards the rail, pointing, and exclaiming in whispers.

Right on the waterline, only yards from the place of my now-confirmed original sighting, was a huge polar bear. The reason that it hadn't moved very far was only too grotesquely evident. It had caught a big seal and was now completely bloodied and preoccupied with devouring its kill on the spot. Having probably stalked the poor creature for hours, maybe days, it was set on going nowhere.

Near at hand there lurked a brave little Arctic fox, who'd occasionally nip in, hyena-like, to steal the odd titbit. Presumably it reckoned that with this much seal meat to be consumed, fox wouldn't be anywhere on today's menu, nor would a few scraps be missed from the busy bear's great banquet.

In near silence we watched the feast on the shoreline. As we did so, we realized that the kill had almost certainly happened in the last hour or so, while we were cruising away towards what had proved to be No Bears Bay. At length we took the last of a hundred photographs and I did a now triumphant piece to our camera.

Before we retired for the night I looked back at the bear's ears. They were now caked in the blood of its kill. But when I'd first seen them, large and white, I knew now they'd been unmistakably those of a polar bear.

Icebergs

One enthralling memory of our trip to Svalbard is the actual sound of the Arctic. You hear very little from most animals, maybe the barking of an Arctic fox or the call of a reindeer. But apart from the seal colonies, or the walrus rookeries, animal sounds are rare.

Birds too are unexpectedly quiet, except perhaps for gulls flocking in a harbour. But although kittiwakes flew the whole time over the wake of our ship, they too were silent.

What we did hear the most, day and night, was the noise of water and ice. During the short summer the air is filled with the sound of melting as the ice is dissolved by the midnight sun, providing a constant soundtrack throughout this stupendous part of the planet. For a few brief weeks summer drips away, until the meltwaters are silenced by the autumn frosts and the whole circle begins again.

Above and next page: Amongst the icebergs.

Right: A spectacular waterfall caused by ice melted by the midnight sun.

Another frequent summertime sound is the huge boom of glaciers falling, sometimes hundreds of feet, to crash into an ice canyon below. Even when you know it's just ice breaking off on an enormous scale it sounds like cannonfire, or someone quarrying way off in the distance. Sometimes, from up towards the Pole, in the small hours of the morning it can be heard from over 50 miles away.

But the most impressive noises came from the icebergs. Until now I had never seen an iceberg and, perhaps like most of us, apart from sitting through the film *Titanic* and being distracted anyway by Kate Winslet, I had never properly appreciated them.

Icebergs were one of the most memorable sights of our entire Arctic adventure. Not only are they huge but, far from being inert lumps of floating snow, I discovered that they were hissing, cracking and reforming all the time. Like the polar bear they are beautiful, they are

White, green and blue are their dominant colours – a bay full of drifting icebergs can seem like an artist's wildest imaginings.

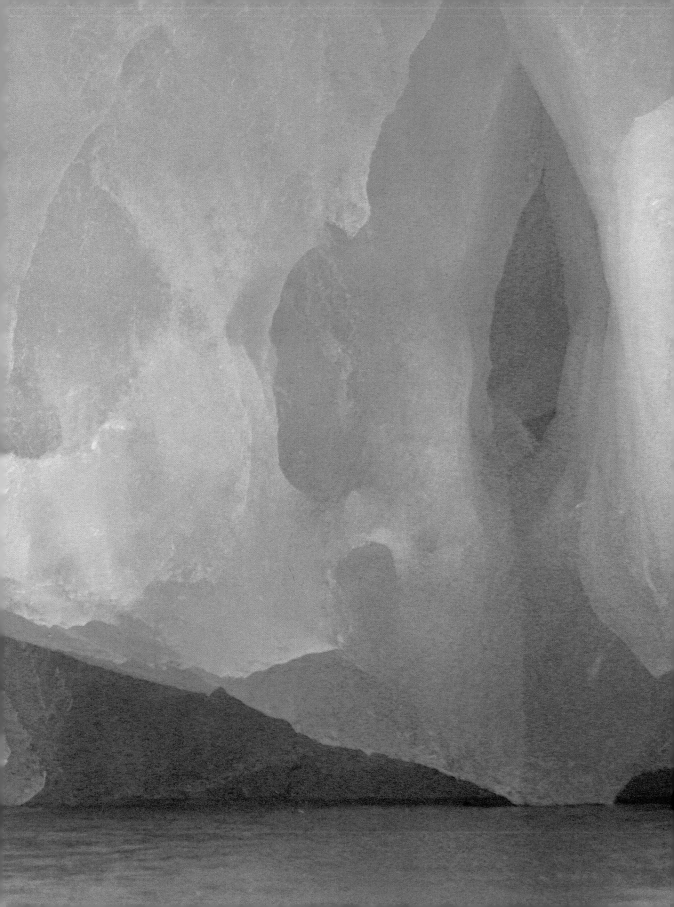

awesome, but they are also very dangerous.

Everyone understands the expression 'just the tip of the iceberg', but only when close up do you get a real sense of what that means. The size of an iceberg, beneath the sea, can be anything between three and nine times as large as the amount exposed above the surface. Sometimes, as we got close – perhaps too close – to some of the bigger icebergs, a huge vortex of water would suddenly be pushed up to the surface. It would be accompanied by a massive chunk of ice that had just broken off, way beneath the ocean.

Icebergs were one of the most memorable sights of our Arctic adventure. I discovered that they were hissing, cracking and reforming all the time. Like the polar bear they are beautiful, they are awesome, but they are also very dangerous.

Eerily beautiful but also very noisy – and highly dangerous.

One terrifying moment came when we were filming on a remote island north of the town of Ny-Ålesund. Without warning there was a loud splintering noise, and 50 yards from the shore an iceberg shattered. As we watched, an enormous slab of the iceberg's summit fell into the sea. Immediately this had the effect of unbalancing the whole towering thing, turning it completely upside down. As it settled in its new form the iceberg showed itself now much taller, with a bright green underside.

One particularly frightening thing then happened. The iceberg's violent re-emergence caused a sudden roaring of water all around our little island like a flood tide. There was an enormous undertow, scattering seals and sending a surge of broken seaweed in every direction. Ripped from its mooring, our little Zodiac was dragged along the shore for 50 yards. Only a frantic grab at the trailing rope by Erik saved us from losing our boat altogether. We knew how lucky this escape had been. This is not a part of the world in which you would want to be marooned.

From this moment on we showed a new respect for areas where icebergs were drifting. Any one of them is colossal. To be a true iceberg they must be at least 17 feet proud of the ocean; anything smaller is rather charmingly called a growler. The one that sank the *Titanic* was reckoned to be 'about six stories above the water'. Another, recorded by scientists off the coast of Greenland, stood over 550 feet clear of the sea. Beneath the surface it must have been the size of Cornwall.

Nor did we expect that icebergs could display such a wonderful range of colours. I'd thought they would be white, white and white. In fact, white, green and blue are their dominant colours and these, plus reflections cast by sun and sea, can make a bay full of drifting icebergs seem like an artist's wildest imaginings.

Where they appear white, they're obviously covered with fresh ice and snow. An iceberg's particular deep rich shade of green is caused by algae, and is only seen when one rolls over, exposing surfaces formerly under water. The blue, reminiscent of the sky, is almost a turquoise. This beautiful effect is caused by all the gas inside being compressed within the ice, to the point that light scattering through the iceberg makes blue its predominant colour.

One strange fact that the Captain told me, one evening as we cruised slowly past some growlers, is that in some parts of the Arctic icebergs are regularly lassooed, to be towed away by ships. This is done mainly in places like Alaska, where they need to be prevented from smashing into oil rigs and drilling platforms. Occasionally they are also taken as a source of drinking water and, how absurd is this ... one Alaskan company harvests icebergs floating in their home waters and sells them to the Japanese. They are then sold on the novelty market, fetching a high price as pieces of genuine iceberg.

The one that sank the *Titanic* was reckoned to be 'about six stories above the water'. Another off the coast of Greenland stood over 550 feet clear of the sea. Beneath the surface it must have been the size of Cornwall.

Right: Getting this close we discovered later was not a good idea...

Next page: Drifting ice and the remains of an iceberg.

During the short summer the air is filled with the sound of melting as the ice is dissolved by the midnight sun, providing a constant soundtrack throughout this stupendous part of the planet..

Bear from the Air

My next encounter with a polar bear is something I'll never forget. We'd been filming all day from the air, above the breathtaking mountains and glaciers of northern Norway's Longyearben area. This awe-inspiring landscape was thickly populated with herds of reindeer and caribou who, without being panicked by us into a stampede, were quick to move away from the shadow of our helicopter and the noise made by its engine.

Having spent a large sum of kroners on hiring the helicopter, we'd hoped that searching from the air would virtually guarantee us the chance to capture at least one other bear on film. By late afternoon, however, we still had not seen hide nor hair of a polar bear. This was particularly disappointing since there are known to be over 2,500 bears in the Svalbard area. According to our pilot though, there was nothing unusual about the apparent absence of any bears, since their sensitivity to noise would let them hear us while we were still some miles away. Also, despite their massive size, they could be extraordinarily good at camouflaging themselves, especially down on the sea ice.

Towards the end of the day our cameraman, harnessed by a tough canvas belt, was still filming, with his legs dangling from the open helicopter door. Suddenly everyone gave a shout. Swimming lazily along the shoreline just beneath us was an enormous male bear. The size of the head, even half submerged in the icy ocean, and the power of the creature's massive legs, made this one of the unforgettable sights of my life.

We were beside ourselves. This wonderful moment is one whose details we still share, back in London, whenever any of us meet up who were there that day. The bear responded to our presence by swimming strongly to the shore. When it emerged and shook itself dry, it resembled a huge, pure white dog.

But then it looked up at us. Its menace was unmistakable. Not wanting to disturb it further, after circling it two or three more times more, we left this awesome creature in peace.

It was one of the
unforgettable sights of
my life. This wonderful
moment is one whose
details we still share.

The Trapper

As our helicopter touched down, we were still ecstatic from our recent aerial sighting of a polar bear. Then, only a few hundred yards around the coast from where we'd spotted the bear, we met the most extraordinary gentleman. He was a trapper, a Mr Arne Solbakken, about 60 years old, married, with three kids back in the south of Norway. With a couple of medium-sized dogs as his only companions and protection, he was happily settling into a flimsy-looking wooden cabin. For the next year of his life this was to be his home – as a test, so we understood, of his inner strength.

Through Erik, our interpreter, he told us, 'I want to find out what kind of man I am.' One member of our crew who should remain nameless – okay, then, let's call him Dave – turned to me and muttered, 'We know what kind of a man you are, mate. You're a nutter.'

It has to be said that if Mr Solbakken was a nutter, he was a very nice one, and positively beamed at us in welcome as we touched down in his icy backyard. Evidently he'd only just arrived himself, to start preparing for the long months ahead. He would have no phone, radio or TV, let alone fax, laptop or emails. For many of us, living in a more stressful but far less dangerous environment, this would be heaven – for a day or two.

He did admit to being concerned about what he described as 'the dark time', the six-month Arctic winter of almost total blackness. Frankly the prospect of living through this time in solitude might make anyone concerned. More worrying yet was the fact that in winter the polar bears would be at their most active. We knew from our own observations that this was serious bear country. In fact we also discovered that earlier in the year this same cabin had been attacked a couple of times and smashed to pieces by polar bears looking for something nice to eat. Enter the very edible Mr Arne Solbakken.

Above and next page: Erik and I say goodbye to Arne. We would be the last company he would have for twelve months – apart from polar bears.

Above right: Arne's isolated cabin from the air.

Below right: Seal meat.

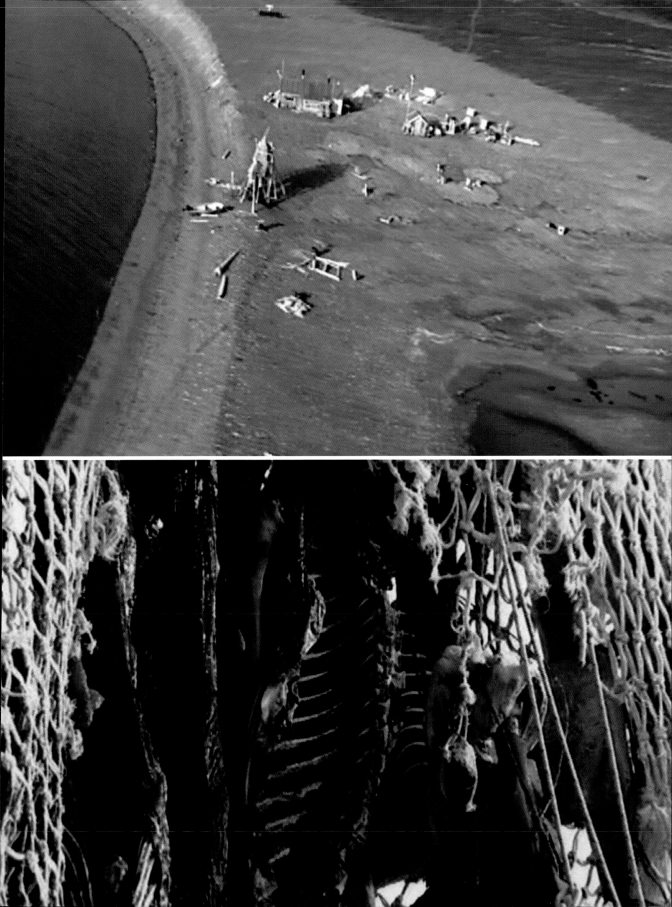

Earlier in the year this same cabin had been attacked a couple of times and smashed to pieces by polar bears looking for something to eat. Enter the very edible Mr Solbakken.

It wasn't as if at the end of all this Arne and his family would gain anything substantial. If he did emerge unscathed, the conquering hero would have no cash reward nor mound of prize gourmet food to take home in triumph. Assuming the family did welcome Arne home a year down the line, and hadn't moved without telling him or changed all the locks, life for the Solbakkens would just go on much as it had before.

The food didn't sound great, either. Arne's staple diet would consist almost entirely of seal, walrus and an occasional ptarmigan. This might

Arne's diet would be almost entirely seal, walrus and ptarmigan. To make doubly sure that Mr Bear couldn't miss him, he had carcasses of walrus and ringed seal hung up drying all around the outside walls of his cabin.

Seal meat is hung all around Arne's cabin, just in case the bears couldn't find him.

be alright as an adventurous one-off. But I doubted that even Nigella Lawson herself could make seal and walrus too varied and exciting three hundred and sixty-five times on the go. Not even with the odd garnish of ptarmigan.

Nor would it have been a good place for a vegetarian: the only greens in evidence were a kind of Arctic heather. Finally, to make doubly sure that Mr Bear couldn't miss him, Arne had great carcasses of walrus and ringed seal, the polar bear's main diet, hung up drying all around the outside walls of his cabin.

It's now been pitch black up on Svalbard since September and I've no idea if Arne is still there. I think probably not. But then no one will know for certain, until the ice melts.

For the next year of his life
this was to be his home –
as a test, so we understood,
of his inner strength.

Erik and Hilda

The idea of testing oneself seems to be a recurring theme amongst the inhabitants of the Arctic, and certainly it is for the Norwegians who live up there. In spite of the bitter temperatures, and the great variation between non-stop daylight and total darkness, they love to be outdoors. They trek through the ice, they camp, they hunt, they skidoo, they run for days with teams of huskies. Though they live in one of the most extreme regions on the planet, they revel in their harsh climate.

Above and right: Erik, our intrepid guide, also mad as a trumpet.

Their hunting is very controlled. Obviously polar bears are completely off limits and each hunter is allowed one reindeer per season. Our guide, Erik, having shot his reindeer at two minutes past midnight on the first day of the season, knew that it would be the only deer he'd be allowed for the rest of the year. But he seemed to accept the fact that throughout the summer he would have to content himself with grouse, foxes and Arctic hares. He was an expert shot and acted for the entire trip as our guide.

However, given all the years he'd guided in this dangerous land, I was somewhat surprised when he confided to me that, 'I have never actually shot a polar bear.' This was because, in his experience, flares and loud noise had always been enough to make any bear move away. So far so good. More alarmingly though, he also said, 'I question myself often and I don't know whether, if I absolutely had to, I would actually be able to shoot a bear in time to save us.' Oh, great.

I really liked Erik. He was a great bloke and a good companion, full of stories and an endless source of information about the animals, plants and glacial formations all around us. But I think we'd have settled for someone altogether more dull as a guide, not to say grumpy, provided we knew that an angry bear with us on his menu would be killed, first shot every time.

Then there was Hilda. In England the name Hilda conjures images of masculine, mature women from a bygone age. It's always seemed apt that Hilda is Margaret Thatcher's middle name. But this Hilda was young, gorgeous, and very feminine – given that she was one tough lady. She drank shoulder to shoulder with the men and enjoyed nothing more after dinner than arm wrestling with the more strapping members of the crew. She too loved to test herself, and apparently so did her husband, even on their honeymoon.

Men and women admittedly can go through all sorts of rigours in those first few nights together. But Hilda had a honeymoon with a difference. The two of them stayed in a remote cabin deep in bear country. They had some food and a rifle, but during what must have been a memorable start to their married life, the newly-weds counted no less than eight polar bears sniffing at their scent from outside their cabin door. At one point there were several bears together growling through the flimsy wooden walls. Oh, and they were in separate bunk beds.

Hilda, who spent her first week of married life in a cabin surrounded by polar bears.

'It was fantastic,' Hilda told me. 'We didn't get a wink of sleep.'

Then there was the swimming. It was made clear to us as we boarded the *Polar Star* that at some point during the trip we would be expected to swim. We made it equally clear to the Captain and crew that this was unlikely, as in out of the question. The sea was bitterly cold – indeed there was ice all around us. In these conditions, what sort of nutter would even contemplate a swim?

The Hilda sort of nutter, of course.

One early evening at Ny Alesund, when the air was full of frost, it was announced that all those who wanted to could swim just off the shore. We English to a man and Geraint as the token Welshman refused point blank to get off even one layer of kit. But barking Hilda led a women's revolt. She, Ingrid, Jean and several of the other women on board bonded together to shame us all and, screaming manically, hurled themselves into the Arctic Ocean.

Understandably they didn't last long, but from the nice warm bar where we watched, it was very impressive. The Captain grinned at us and said, rightly enough, 'The sea is full of revolting women.' My wife Ingrid emerged glowing, with goose pimples in places where I didn't know she had places, and we men felt almost ashamed. 'Almost' because nothing would have made us put even a toe into that icy-looking water.

As an experiment the skipper took the temperature of the ocean at that point. It was minus 1.5 degrees. At minus 2 the sea freezes over ...

Our guide Erik was an expert shot and acted as our guide. Alarmingly though, he also said, 'I question myself often and I don't know whether, if I absolutely had to, I would actually be able to shoot a bear in time to save us.' Oh, great.

Funny people, these Norwegians. I should know – I'm married to one. Their ambiguous attitude to the local climate was summed up by the latest joke doing the rounds in Svalbard when we were there.

A baby bear is heard asking his mother if he really is a polar bear. Mother says, 'Of course you are a polar bear. You have a black nose and lovely, fluffy white fur. Your mummy is a polar bear, your daddy is a polar bear, your granddad was a polar bear, your great-great-granddad was a polar bear. Of course you are a polar bear.'

Father polar bear wanders across and says, 'As your mother has told you, of course you are a polar bear. But what makes you ask?' The baby polar bear replies, 'Because I am absolutely bloody freezing!...'

My wife Ingrid emerged glowing, and we men almost felt ashamed. 'Almost' because nothing would have made us put even a toe into that icy-looking water.

The Bear in the Sea

We kept on looking, without success. Then suddenly it happened: we were rowing in our tiny Zodiac inflatable boat, some distance from our ship, only to be confronted by an enormous male polar bear. It had reared up from behind a rock, seemingly out of nowhere, to see who on earth we were. It came to the water's edge and stared at us for a while and then got into the sea and started purposefully swimming in the direction of our boat until it was no more than 20 yards away from us.

We spoke in whispers, mesmerized, but also terrified. Miraculously it decided to give us no more than an aggressive warning, bellowing and hissing at us, noises that echoed and magnified from the glaciers all around. We were told later that they were heard more than a mile away on the main ship and they knew that we must be in trouble. Mercifully, once it had told us very clearly to back off from its territory, it turned and swam effortlessly across to the far shore.

It was only after it had gone that we saw we'd been in greater danger than we had realized. As, hugely elated but still almost trembling from what we had just experienced, we turned the Zodiac to row back to the main ship, one of our stubby oars touched the bottom and we realized that all the time the huge bear had been swimming towards us it was in water no more than 3 or 4 feet deep. It could have reared up at any moment and smashed our frail boat, and us, to pieces.

> **We were told later that the bear's bellows and hisses were heard more than a mile away on the main ship and they knew we must be in trouble. Mercifully, he turned and swam.**

Right: Because of rigid conservation laws, the *Polar Star* had to stay 300 yards off the shoreline. To get closer we had to get into our little inflatable.

Next page: Our too-close encounter.

He could have reared
up at any moment and
smashed our frail boat,
and us, to pieces.

3
IN THE KINGDOM OF THE POLAR BEAR

Bears Swimming

Twice during our expedition we were lucky enough to have the extraordinary sight of these huge creatures making their way through the icy sea. As swimmers in the freezing Arctic waters, polar bears can show formidable strength and endurance. This helps them move around in search of food, even when they may have to swim for hours at a time over long distances in order to find a new seal habitat on the frozen ocean. Scientists have tracked individual bears capable of swimming without a break for over 62 miles. During journeys like these the bears can move through the water at a speed of over 6 miles an hour.

The actual swimming style of the polar bear is a vigorous doggy paddle. The bear propels itself through the water with strong movements of its front legs, whose five-toed paws help by being partly webbed and have an enormous, almost disproportionate, diameter of up to 12 inches.

As hunters, polar bears have adapted to spend as much time on ice as they do on land. When stalking their prey on the ice floes, they frequently use a shallow diving technique. Their efficiency as divers is helped by their excellent underwater vision, which enables them to spot a seal from as far away as 15 feet. Bears usually swim at depths of 10 or 12 feet, which they do with their nostrils closed. Although they can't venture much below about 20 feet, they can stay submerged for at least two minutes. When a polar bear climbs back out of the sea, it can dry itself very quickly. Its fur, being oily, is water repellent, and the hairs don't matt when wet. This allows the bear to shake itself free of water or any ice that may become attached after swimming. Ice can otherwise form very quickly when the animal's wet fur is exposed to air temperatures of zero degrees or less.

For thousands of seals each summer, the last thing they ever see is one of these massive creatures bursting up from the ocean as if from nowhere. As we explored in our tiny inflatable boat, it was impossible not to feel the terror of this constantly at the back of our minds.

Capable of swimming long distances and with excellent underwater vision, bears can get uncomfortably close to inflatables...

For thousands of seals, the last thing they ever see is one of these massive creatures bursting up from the ocean. In our small boat it was impossible not to feel the terror of this.

Bears Catching Their Food

Polar bears feed on whatever is available in the Arctic wastes. This varies from region to region and includes reindeer, foxes, small rodents, various kinds of seabird, ducks, fish, eggs, berries, grasses, kelp, and human garbage when they can get it, sometimes scavenging in large numbers. And of course, on mercifully rare occasions, they eat humans.

The bears' most plentiful food source is ringed and bearded seals. And of course, on mercifully rare occasions, they eat humans.

A bearded seal, the bears' most common prey.

But the most plentiful food source is ringed and bearded seals, with harp or hooded seal on the side. When necessary they will scavenge the carcasses of whales, belugas, narwhals and bowheads and even walruses. In fact a dead walrus, a massive 2.5-ton feast, can attract a large number of bears from several miles around. Alive, the fully grown animal is a very different and dangerous prospect. Young walruses, not yet fully grown, are often attacked as are young beluga whales. When no other food is available, bears will eat their own cubs, the male tracking the mother and her cubs relentlessly until they are exhausted and one succumbs.

A polar bear's stomach in happy hunting grounds can hold up to 20 per cent of its body weight. As with humans, about half of all they eat is used to keep them warm. However, polar bears do not need to drink water, but get all the liquid they need from their food. An individual needs to catch at least one seal a week or its equivalent in order to survive. In a single meal a bear can often eat as much as a hundred pounds of seal blubber. And each bear catches an estimated 50–75 seals a year, travelling hundreds of miles to track the seals to their feeding grounds, the icy areas where the ringed seals are thickest in numbers. These can alter from year to year as the ice moves around with each changing season.

The ringed seal, a short, plump creature, is the most numerous and widely distributed marine mammal in the Arctic. Filming from the air we saw hundreds of them, lying in packs where they had hauled themselves out of the icy water. They seemed extremely sensitive to any disturbance, diving when the helicopter approached overhead. Huge numbers of ringed seals means they are also killed in large numbers by Inuit hunters and in many native settlements provide not just their food but also the whole basis of the local economy. They provide nourishment also for Arctic foxes, wolverines, walruses and even ravens. But it is the polar bear which is their main enemy, their chief predator.

In spite of their very large number of enemies the ringed seals are estimated to number as many as six million in the Arctic and are easily the most abundant of the Arctic seals. Like polar bears their young are born in dens which the female digs out of the snow. This shelter helps to provide safety from predators as well as protection from the bitterly cold Arctic winds. But the polar bear's extraordinary sense of smell, and its amazing ability, for such a massive animal, to move slowly and quietly when hunting makes the young seals very vulnerable, even in their hideaways under

The bear's extraordinary sense of smell, and its amazing ability, for such a massive animal, to move slowly and quietly when hunting, makes young seals very vulnerable.

the snow. A bear can scent a seal, deep in its den, from more than half a mile away. Out in the open it can smell one from a distance of over 20 miles. In springtime, when the mother bear needs to feed her cubs, stalking seals in their birth lairs hidden under the snow is their preferred hunting method. Both the mother seal and her newborn pups shelter there and both have the high fat content that the bear requires to feed her own family.

**Mr Bear's breakfast.
A bear needs one seal
a week to survive...**

Watching the bear in action is extraordinary to observe. Once the bear identifies a seal's birth lair it moves incredibly quietly, positioning itself close by. It will repeatedly sniff the air, smelling the young seals and their mother through the ice. Once it has fixed by its acute sense of smell that it is directly over the lair it silently raises itself up on its massive hind legs

The polar bear is an extraordinarily patient hunter. It will wait, motion-less, sometimes for several hours beside one of the seals' regular breathing holes.

A bear lying in wait, its
distinctive black nose
disguised with snow.

and then crashes down with its front paws to break through the roof.
Sometimes several smashing blows are needed before it can break the
hard ice surface of the roof.

The polar bear is an extraordinarily patient hunter. It will wait, motion-
less, sometimes for several hours beside one of the seals' regular
breathing holes. Having crept up to the hole the bear will lie flat on its
stomach and chest with its chin on the ice waiting for a seal to appear.
According to Inuit observers they have been seen covering their black
noses with snow to make them even less detectable. Seals have a number
of such holes in the ice where they will come up for air. When the seal
surfaces the bear attacks, seizing it by the head and flipping the seal onto
the ice where it devours it.

They use the same sort of patient technique for hunting seals that are
already out of the water, lying in packs on the sea ice. As well as having
remarkable senses of smell and sight, polar bears also have the advantage
of hearing at least as sensitive as in humans. Once it has spotted its victim,
the bear will slowly and steadily stalk it until it is about 20 yards away.
Then it will charge at amazing speed, grabbing the animal with claws and
teeth before it can react.

The energy required to chase down prey explains the polar bear's pref-
erence for the kind of hunting that requires it to keep still for much of
the time. A static bear expends thirteen times less energy than one who is
walking, let alone running. Polar bears rarely charge after snow geese, for
example, even when passing though a colony thick with them. The math-
ematics of doing so are incontrovertible, since a dash among the birds for
as little as twelve seconds would readily use more calories than the bear
would gain by catching one.

Polar bears will also stalk seals from the water. The bears are virtually
amphibious, are equally at home in the sea and swim almost silently. They
can disappear under water for minutes at a time and once within range of
their prey they rear out of the water and seize the seal before it can
escape. After feeding on a seal a bear will almost invariably nap for an
hour or more. When charging seals or being chased by hunters they can
run as fast as 25 miles an hour for short distances. Such a sprint will tend
not to last long because of the danger of overheating. More often the
walking speed of a polar bear is about 3.5 miles an hour.

Largely to conserve energy, most polar bears will sleep for about the same length of time as humans, for seven to eight hours at a time. They're likely to sleep more during the day because it is at night that seals tend to be more active. This is certainly true of the spring and summer months – although in Arctic regions 'day' and 'night' mean very little, during summer's endless daylight and the corresponding darkness of winter.

Considering the number of enemies that the ringed seal has it is amazing that it continues to survive in such huge numbers. To the coastal Inuit, it is an essential part of their very existence. In addition to eating the meat and the blubber as part of their staple diet (doesn't sound too good, does it?) they make tents, mats and clothing from the skin and tools from the seal's bones. They burn the fat for warmth and light in the depths of the Arctic winter. And they even make the seal's intestines, stretched transparent, into igloo windows.

The range of the bear is circumpolar, crossing any national border within the extent of the sea ice, and a single polar bear may rove across an area twice as big as Iceland. One Alaskan polar bear's territory was found to be forty-five times the size of Tennessee's Great Smokey Mountain National Park. To put this into perspective, the park supports over four hundred black bears. Polar bears living in areas of sea ice with an abundance of seals do of course have a smaller home range.

Though it's agreed that most polar bears will limit their travels to within a range of a few hundred square miles, some exceptions are astonishing. One satellite-tracked female amazed researchers by trekking for a distance in excess of 3,000 miles. Starting from Prudhoe Bay, Alaska, it crossed the top of the world to Greenland, and spent the winter on Canada's Ellesmere Island before travelling yet again to Greenland. Ignorant of what a famous bear it had become, it was observed through every inch of its extraordinary journey.

Right: Mother and cub asleep.

Next page: A bear crosses an icefield during the spring thaw.

In Inuit legend the polar bear is always the lonely one or the great traveller. A single bear may rove across an area as big as Iceland.

Bears Feasting

The polar bear is a powerful but solitary figure. Apart from mating or a mother looking after her young cubs, they are mainly loners and woe betide any other bear in their path. They travel hundreds of miles and seem happy to do so. In Inuit legend the polar bear is always the lonely one or the great lone traveller.

But there are times when there are great comings together of polar bears in order to feed. This is not a good time for a puny human to get in the way, but the very few lucky scientists to have witnessed it say it is a truly awesome spectacle.

Some massive food source like a dead walrus or a whale carcass will attract polar bears with their acute sense of smell from many miles around. Sometimes a dozen or even more bears will join in the feast for days and nights until virtually nothing remains.

Sometimes a whole pod of beluga whales or narwhals gets trapped in an area of ice, and polar bears join forces to herd them. Then an orgy of killing and eating will begin.

A pod of beluga whales.

One Russian eye-witness has described perhaps as many as a hundred polar bears packed around the colossal carcass of a grey whale off the coast of northern Russia, and in the same area observed fourteen male bears eating shoulder to shoulder at the corpse of an adult walrus. Polar bears have jagged back teeth and large, sharp canines, but characteristically they swallow their food in large chunks rather than bother to do any chewing.

Sometimes a whole pod of beluga whales or narwhals gets trapped inside a reducing area of ice, and polar bears join forces to herd them into an area where they become stranded. Then an orgy of killing and eating will begin.

One such massacre was observed just a few years ago off the coast of Canada's Ellesmere Island, when at least fifty belugas were trapped and devoured over many days by polar bears. And, of course, for the huge bears, something like this is a vast calorie intake with minimal energy used. It's the perfect kill as a single narwhal can weigh over 2,600 pounds. There is a real etiquette to these orgies of feeding and it seems that on the beach the polar bears are much more generous and happy to share a kill than they normally might be. They appear to show a much higher tolerance of other male bears than they do further inland or on the ice. But even so there is a real pecking order.

Some massive food source like a dead walrus or a whale carcass will attract polar bears with their acute sense of smell from many miles around. Sometimes a dozen or more will join in and feast for days.

The male who first found the kill has to accept the others who arrive. There is a strange begging behaviour from the joining bears, a submissive low to the ground approach, usually followed by some nose touching. When they are all feeding together there is a lot of growling and snorting. It is very similar to many other animals who come together for a kill, like lions and wolves. The females and cubs have to wait their turn though and by the time they're all done it's left to the foxes and the gulls to pick at the bones. There is a rather grisly side benefit to this joint feeding. It is a lot easier for the bears collectively to rip open a carcass. Walrus skin can be so tough it often takes even a fully grown male bear two or three hours to rip his way into the meat inside, so groups will often join forces to tear open the carcass of a big dead walrus around the genitals where the skin is softer and then take turns to slowly enlarge the hole. I just thought I'd share that with you.

Right: Unwanted dinner guests. A bear guards its kill from scavenging gulls.

Next page: There is a benefit to sharing...

There is a grisly side benefit to the joint feeding. Groups will tear open the carcass of a walrus around the genitals where the skin is softer and then take turns to enlarge the hole. I just thought I'd share that with you.

The Walrus

As we approached the bare flat gravel of Moffin Island our skipper cut the engines, in order to keep us the obligatory 300 yards offshore. During the walrus breeding season this was as close as you could get to the island, which was completely covered in these massive animals. It's been one of their regular breeding grounds for centuries, visited by them in huge numbers every year between May and September. Many tend to remain there all year round, even in the winter when the area ices over, making them much more vulnerable to attack from polar bears.

Left and above: Moffin Island, a regular breeding ground for walruses.

The walruses seemed really happy to see us, diving off rocks and coming up right underneath our boat in an elaborate game of hide and seek. Although the large adult animals don't have much to fear they tend nonetheless to stay together like this for safety against polar bears. From time to time the bears are seen trying to approach Moffin Island, but in the main they are beaten off by the sheer numbers and aggression of the walruses. A full-sized walrus is probably the only animal that can resist the attack of a polar bear. Their skin is as tough as an armoured car and their tusks are vicious.

Polar bears will regularly feast on a large dead walrus, often feeding several at a time, since the smell of the carcass can attract a number of bears from miles around. They will certainly attack a live young walrus if they can get it away from its parents. Usually though, they will only turn to walruses as a possible food item if they are really hungry.

Some of the animals we saw on Moffin Island were enormous. A big walrus can weigh more than one ton and grow to over 14 feet long. Bears and humans are their only enemy although like the polar bear they too are now protected from commercial hunters. The natives in the Arctic regions are still allowed to take a regulated number of walruses every year for food, and the oil from the animals' carcasses is used for lighting and heating Inuit homes. The skin too is used, to make clothing or bedding. The tusks can be fashioned as hunting spears and revoltingly enough the walruses' intestines are much prized for making raincoats!

Walruses are sociable animals. On Moffin Island we saw several hundred, diving into the sea and pulling themselves back up onto the rocks with their tusks. They are also enormously strong. Although on land they are clumsy and slow-moving, in water they can move very fast. They live almost entirely on clams, which are found buried on the sea bed. In the course of seeking out food, walruses can squirt high-powered jets of water out of their mouths with such force that this drills out the clams from under the mud. They can dive to the sea bottom at depths of up to 300 feet, and a feasting walrus can eat as many as 4,000 clams in a single sitting.

The walrus's famously thick moustache comprises as many as 700 hairs growing on its nose. This sensitive organ is of course used to sniff out food, but it also seems to be used for nuzzle kissing other walruses. As we watched the Moffin Island walruses, it was clear to see what affectionate creatures they were, from all the nuzzling that was going on. As part of their sexual equipment the tusks were clearly important too, as the males were unmistakably using them to hang on to the female during some impressive feats of mating.

A full-sized walrus is probably the only animal that can resist the attack of a polar bear. Their skin is as tough as an armoured car and their tusks are vicious. Bears are often beaten off by their aggression.

A walrus close up is a fearsome sight.

Walruses are sociable animals. Although the large adults don't have much to fear they tend to stay together like this for safety against polar bears.

Mother and Baby

Two cubs play by their sleeping mother.

For the female polar bear, I'm not sure that the male is much of a catch. I know it's the little things that can make or break a relationship, such as squeezing the wrong end of the toothpaste. But with the male polar bear as a mate it's the big things that stand out. When hungry he'll frequently stalk his own cubs in order to kill and eat them. And not only is he not even slightly monogamous, but he has been recorded and photographed mating with a female that hours before had been shot dead by hunters.

By contrast the female is an extremely careful parent, protective of her cubs and fiercely aggressive towards any other animal, man included, who comes too close to her precious brood. At such a time she is one of the most dangerous of animals, and many terrifying attacks have been a result of man foolishly venturing too near a mother bear. There have even been cases of a female rearing up at a helicopter flying just that bit too low and too close to her cubs.

Competition for females is often a savage affair, with vicious fights breaking out. Fights between rival males are spectacular, each bear lowering his head, flattening back his ears and giving a series of hisses and roars before thundering to the attack.

Surprisingly, these contests are rarely fatal, although they often result in broken teeth or deep scars on the head, neck and shoulders. Perhaps the greatest danger is that in the long hungry winters such injuries can seriously affect the male bear's ability to stalk and hunt his prey, making starvation a real possibility.

The actual mating takes place on the sea ice, around April or May after preliminaries that may carry on for a week or more. For example one keen randy male has been recorded following the tracks of a particular female for more than 60 miles before mating with her. However, from this point on the father has nothing to do with the female bear, nor with his offspring. The male polar bear's back to hunting out on the ice, but only to feed himself, and is soon apt to mate with other females. It's left to the mother to bring up the babies, to protect them and ultimately to teach them how to hunt for themselves.

Although mating takes place in spring, the fertile ova are not implanted until much later in the year. The female bear feeds heavily throughout the summer, putting on as much as 400 pounds in weight, to gain the strength and energy she needs for the months ahead of nursing and feeding her young. Most of this food comes from seal meat, whose calories are the best possible source of the milk needed by her cubs. Only at this point, probably in the month of October, is she ready to give birth. The pregnant sow will then dig her den, usually in a snowdrift, with a ventilation hole in the roof to provide fresh air for herself and her new family. It is here, around Christmas, that she will give birth, in the deepest, darkest part of the long Arctic winter.

A polar bear tends to produce a litter of two or sometimes three cubs. Overall she will breed probably no more than four or five times. She is unlikely to be ready to repeat this amazing and gruelling cycle within at least a further three years.

Mother and cubs will stay within the shelter of the den while the babies pile on weight. She is wonderfully attentive, nuzzling and grooming her young.

At birth, baby polar bears are tiny beautiful creatures no more than about 12 inches long, covered with short soft fur, and weighing only a pound or so. They are extremely vulnerable, being blind and toothless. Mother and cubs will stay within the shelter of the den until at least March or April while the babies pile on weight. Remarkably, during that time the mother bear will not eat, drink or even defecate. She is wonderfully attentive, nuzzling and grooming her young and feeding them several times a day from her own excess calories. The cubs have to grow fast, so that they can be ready to join the hunt before their mother's reserves are exhausted. For this reason a polar bear produces milk richer than that of any other bear, and ten times as rich as human milk.

By the first three or four weeks of life, the baby bears will have grown enough to have opened their eyes. Within the limits of the snow den they will begin to walk during the first two months. When they eventually

A mother bear peers from her den as she waits for her cubs to grow.

make their way into the outside world, usually around March or April, the cubs will already weigh more than 30 pounds. But the young family will stay close to the den for another ten or twelve days before they feel safe enough to explore further afield. This gives them time to acclimatize to the bitter cold and develop their muscles for the long walks ahead as hunters.

When she judges that they are ready, the mother will lead her cubs to the sea ice in search of seals. This is a tough time for the newly emerged bears, who travel slowly with frequent halts for rest and feeding. Through any areas of water or thick snow the mother will carry the cubs on her back. They will begin to eat solid food as soon as she makes her first kill. In the mean time starvation is always a threat, as are attacks by hungry males. A bear that has travelled a long distance without finding food is a particularly dangerous creature.

The female is protective of her precious brood. She is one of the most dangerous animals.

Left and next page: Cubs newly emerged from their den are closely guarded by their mother.

Females will stay with their cubs on average for two and a half years. Nonetheless, there are many fatalities: six out of ten polar bears die in their first year. Also, though in the main the female polar bear is an excellent mother, hungry sows have been known to kill one or even more of their own cubs. But if the young bears do survive and the seals are plentiful, life for the fast-growing cubs can be good. By the age of eight months they will already have grown to over 100 pounds in weight. At this stage their development is almost entirely down to their mother's skill at hunting, even though they have been learning to hunt, by watching her. This is a busy time for her, since in order for all her family to survive she needs to kill at least two seals a week.

Although few young bears catch anything much in their first year, by the time they are two they will be killing a seal about every five or six days. At this point they will be about to move on and start fending for themselves. The mother too, by the third year, may well feel the need to breed once more.

If the young bears do survive
and the seals are plentiful,
life for fast-growing cubs can
be good. By the time they are
two they will be killing a seal
about every five or six days.

Hunting Polar Bears

In spite of the threats posed by pollution and global warming, the greatest danger to the polar bear's very existence has always been hunting. Man has always hunted bears, along with killing just about every other sort of creature. Evidence of bear hunting has been found among the ruins of settlements dating back at least a thousand years. Polar bears have long been hunted for food by native peoples of the Arctic, who also used their pelts for clothes and bedding. Commercial hunting started around the sixteenth century and two centuries later it was flourishing. The killing increased to the point where in the 1950s and 1960s it was on a massive scale. Methods used have included shooting, trapping and poisoning. Spring guns were for a long time probably the most commonly used means. Individual hunters would each set several guns, which they usually baited with a piece of seal or whale blubber. This was connected to the trigger, so that as the bears tugged at the meat, they were shot. Usually they were hit in the head, but depending on the angle from which the bear took the bait, many were indiscriminately wounded, maybe escaping only to die a lingering death from starvation. The spring gun also didn't distinguish between males and females, or even cubs. When mothers with young were shot, the cubs starved to death since, being too young to hunt, they had no chance of survival. Other orphaned cubs might be captured by trappers and sold to zoos.

> **Evidence of bear hunting has been found among the ruins of settlements dating back at least a thousand years. Polar bears have long been hunted by native peoples of the Arctic.**

Never travel alone in the Arctic without a gun.

Other early hunting devices included a pole with bait suspended from it within rifle range of a cabin. From behind the cabin door the trapper would shoot the bear as it took the bait. This was extremely hazardous for the hunter himself, because of the bear's strong sense of smell.

Frequently too the bear wasn't killed outright, making it extremely dangerous. Steel bear traps were also used, but even many hardened bear trappers took the view that these were hideously cruel.

The hunting of polar bears has always been a brutal, bloody business. Even though people should have known better, sickening things have been done to these animals, particularly in the name of sport. Moreover the killing continues.

Perhaps the most degrading means of killing bears for sport was the use of poison. This method was banned altogether in 1927 by international agreement. Nevertheless for many years afterwards bear poison was still sold to hunters in many places throughout the Arctic. Using it was an imprecise and ugly business. The length of time that a bear took to die, having discovered and swallowed a poisoned bait, could vary from a few seconds to five or ten agonizing minutes, depending on whether the bait was frozen, or how much it was chewed before being swallowed. The details of the

Hunting polar bears has always been a brutal, bloody business. Sickening things have been done, particularly in the name of sport. Moreover the killing continues.

bear's death also depended on how much went straight into the stomach. Sometimes the bear would vomit up the bait as soon as it tasted the poison. It might then walk hundreds of yards before collapsing and dying regardless. A tiny number of polar bears are actually known to have survived, presumably because they spat out the poisoned bait in time. Thousands, however, were fated to suffer a slow agonizing death.

Hunters eventually stopped using poison, not on humanitarian grounds, but because too many bears got far enough away to die on the ice, where their bodies were inaccessible. Alternatively many carcasses of poisoned bears failed to be recovered because the animals had disappeared, to die in agony in deep snow.

Among rich sportsmen, so called, in the 1950s the fashion for polar bear safaris became widespread. Some wealthy tourists hired ships used by the local seal-hunters. Others in search of trophies to take home would charter aeroplanes or helicopters in which to pursue the bears. Most of these safaris took place in the summer months. At this season the sea ice was melting and drifting, with the result that bears were easy prey, especially once the chartered seal-hunters' boats became powered by steam or diesel. Once sighted, if the ice was broken up and drifting the bear had no choice but to swim between the ice floes. This left it easily caught up with, so that hunters could shoot at it from any nearby boat. If a bear took refuge on an ice floe, a vessel's whole crew would go ashore to shoot the terrified creature. Either way, in open pack ice polar bears had little hope of escape.

By the 1920s in Svalbard alone, 900 bears died each year. If in the 1970s hunting had not been outlawed, it is probable that the polar bear would now be virtually extinct.

The summer hunting season also saw the capture of a lot of cubs. The female bear was chased into the water and shot, and her young were put into cages. Most of these cubs were sold to zoos or private collectors but many more went straight to the taxidermist.

Inevitably, throughout much of the last century, the polar bear population dwindled. By the 1920s in the Svalbard archipelago alone, more than 900 bears were killed each year. Half a century later, before the introduction of a hunting ban, there were reckoned to be less than 1,000 bears in the whole area. If in the 1970s hunting had not been outlawed, it is probable that the polar bear would now be virtually extinct. In the early part of the decade the use of aircraft or motorized boats for hunting was eventually banned throughout the Arctic. The real breakthrough came in 1973 when Norway and Russia completely banned all polar bear hunting and Canada, Greenland and the United States each introduced a quota system. In the USA polar bears may only be hunted by native Alaskans. Under this law there is no actual limit on the number that may be taken, but for the most part only male bears are killed, and it seems that the law is mostly followed in a responsible way. Canada's quota system is divided among its scattered native communities. Surprisingly, however, in such an environmentally conscious nation, it is the only

country in the world that still allows a degree of trophy hunting for polar bears. Mostly this is carried out by rich Americans. In some cases huge sums of money are paid by these hunters to native Canadians who sell on their own permits.

Although Russia's no-hunting ban is absolute, in such a massive country this would be hard to implement in any circumstances, particularly in the far east, which shares its polar bear population with Alaska, across the Bering Strait. Currently, however, the problem of protecting the bears in that part of Russian is made worse by a general breakdown in law and order. Precise numbers are hard to obtain, but according to Russian government figures, last year in Russia alone 250 polar bears were poached and killed.

Bringing the remaining slaughter to a stop is bound to be difficult. But the last thirty years have seen a series of international agreements that have reversed the decline in the world population of polar bears.

Careful control of hunting is still essential, even though the polar bear population is classified as 'threatened' rather than 'endangered'. Numbers around the Arctic as a whole are hard to assess. Scientific guesstimates of how many polar bears are left throughout the world range from 16,000 up to as many as 35,000. Currently general agreement has settled on a figure of about 22,000. What is certain is that the numbers have greatly increased since hunting became regulated, at a time when the world polar bear population was down to less than 10,000.

Left: A polar bear is skinned and stretched out to dry.

Bringing the remaining slaughter to a stop is bound to be difficult. But the last thirty years have at least seen a series of international agreements succeed in reversing the decline in the world population of polar bears. Public attitudes, too, have come a long way since the 1920s, when in a single day's 'sport' on the Svalbard islands a Captain Peder Ulssjord shot forty bears, but bemoaned the fact that too many others escaped his rifle.

The Governor's Office

The Sysselmannen, the Governor of the province of Svalbard, has complete control over the shooting of polar bears. There is a simple rule: you are only allowed to shoot a polar bear if your life is threatened. All cases where polar bears are shot are investigated by the police and a large fine is imposed if a bear is killed or injured except in self-defence. And even then if the situation was indeed life-threatening but was prompted by provocative or dangerous behaviour, a prosecution will also follow.

The decision to shoot any bear is made by the Sysselmannen and if any bear is shot he must immediately be informed. Likewise anyone who is not in immediate danger but has reason to suspect that a bear attack is likely must also contact the Governor's office. This occurs commonly when bears get too close to scientific research stations and show regular signs of aggression.

Conflicts between humans and bears usually fall into three groups:

1) Bears destroying human property. This is quite common but compensation is rarely given as it is seen as an accepted risk for anyone setting up home in an area populated by polar bears. Because of this lack of financial redress a lot of incidents are not reported. People just shrug and rebuild their shattered cabins, until the next time.

2) Bears threatening people, dogs or property. In most of these cases the bears are chased away with no harm done. But occasionally these incidents end up with the bear having to be shot.

3) Bears killing or injuring people. This is very rare but it can and does happen.

Statistics show that although the number of bears has increased significantly since hunting was outlawed in 1973, there are overall fewer serious confrontations today between man and bear than in the seventies. A widespread program of bear public awareness from the Governor's office has taught an increasing number of people how to be aware of and avoid dangerous situations.

Most of the advice from the Governor's office is very straightforward, even obvious, but many people ignore these simple guidelines.

Before you start walking in any area where you might encounter polar bears, make sure that you have adequate equipment to scare bears off as well as a heavy duty rifle. A smaller calibre weapon may only serve to make a polar bear angry. Make sure you can operate the weapon and always have the gun close by you either in your tent or with you whenever you go for a walk. Check the gun regularly to avoid malfunction as a jam or a misfire could well prove fatal.

Statistics show that although the number of bears has increased significantly since hunting was outlawed in 1973, there are overall fewer serious confrontations today with man than in the seventies.

Some areas are more prone to polar bear activity than others. Avoid camping in any area which is known to have regular polar bear encounters. For example, polar bears often follow the shoreline both in summer and winter and any camp should be some distance away from the shore, preferably with a good view in all directions.

Don't ever camp near polar bear feeding dens or any areas with lots of polar bear tracks. If you are camping, you should try and erect some sort of detection system, trip wires are readily available for this purpose all over Svalbard. Also well-trained dogs are excellent for detection. They can detect polar bears from a long distance away, although one real danger is that if the bear approaches from down wind, the dog may not pick up the scent of the bear until it's too late.

Next page: The skull of an adult bear shows the size of its teeth.

Another suggestion for groups of campers in remote areas is to have a revolving guard system where each person in the camp stays awake for an hour or two throughout the night. At such times as the solitary sentry you can feel terribly alone, but the system works.

Bears are often attracted by food or rubbish at campsites or cabins. Polar bears visiting waste dumps near scientific settlements are a problem

All cases where polar bears are shot are investigated by the police and a large fine is imposed if a bear is killed or injured except in self-defence.

throughout the Arctic. When camping waste should be stored some distance away from the main campsite and in a spot where it can be easily monitored.

Remember bears have an extraordinary sensitive nose that can smell food from a long distance away. It is essential to hide any food away from sleeping tents and in a way that makes it difficult for the bears to get to it. Try to put the food into plastic boxes to reduce the scent and always keep vigilant when cooking food out in the open. Never try to attract polar bears with food as a way of getting them closer to take photographs and never, ever feed them. Ignore your childhood memories of Yogi Bear, the simple reality is that bears that get too familiar with people can become extremely dangerous.

Here are a few stories from the files of confrontations with polar bears in recent years. Some had happy endings, some did not.

Two men who chased a polar bear with snowmobiles in an attempt to photograph it were fined heavily by the Svalbard court and also given a twenty-one-day suspended sentence for being drunk in charge of a snowmobile.

Three polar bears, a mother and her two cubs felt by authorities to have become dangerous had to be shot dead by Norwegian police after breaking into at least ten cabins on an island. They apparently broke windows to smash their way into the cabins to get at the food that they could smell from miles away.

A Canadian man on his way home from a movie late one night suddenly came face to face with a polar bear. Knowing that running away would almost certainly prove fatal he stood absolutely still and, showing extraordinary courage and composure, allowed the bear to come right up and sniff him. It then ignored him and went on its way.

A seven-year-old Canadian boy arrived an hour too early for Sunday school and while waiting was found on the church doorstep by a hungry polar bear. The little boy rolled up into a little ball and miraculously escaped with only slight scratches through his heavy jacket.

A Canadian tourist driving along in a four-by-four had his window open photographing seabirds when a bear grabbed his arm. The guide repeatedly punched the bear in the head until it eventually let go and raced the man to hospital. He survived but the arm was virtually torn off.

Four teenage boys were hunting for ptarmigan with a .22 rifle when they walked straight into a polar bear. All the boys ran off except for one who tried to hide among the undergrowth. The bear knocked him unconscious with its huge paws and although the others fired over the bears head and shot it from close range in the leg it continued to savage the boy on the ground, shaking him like a rag doll. It was chased off by his parents who somehow got themselves between the bear and the unconscious boy and, yelling and brandishing logs, finally convinced it to move away. The boy was rushed to hospital and did eventually recover although he needed 129 stitches to the wounds on his head.

A research station on Svalbard had regular visits from inquisitive polar bears and used hand grenades to scare them away. This seems a little extreme although it did the trick until January 1995 when one male polar bear took the grenade in its mouth. The grenade exploded with predictable results.

A hunter who spent the winter with his wife and two daughters in a remote cabin shot a polar bear with his magnum .357. The family discovered when they came back from sledging that a bear had been on their property. The hunter locked his family in the main cabin area and quietly hunted around the rest of the utility and storage areas. When he entered a storage room the bear put its head in through a small window and the hunter shot him. This killing was considered lawful because the hunter was deemed to have felt his family was at risk. The case caused considerable controversy however and many thought the decision should have gone the other way.

In Van Mijen Fjord a guide with no proper training in polar bear threats and without appropriate warning equipment (she had a rifle but little else) shot a bear which approached her and the three tourists who she was taking on a walking tour. The guide had seen the polar bear approach but did nothing to try and scare the bear away before she shot it when it was 25 yards from them. The tour operator was fined 10,000 kroner for breaking the law by not having given the guide the necessary training and equipment for scaring off polar bears.

These are just some of the examples that the Sysselmann's office and other authorities around the Arctic have to deal with every year. In most cases, it is the human that has been at fault.

The Last Two Deaths

It had been a hard, bitter cold winter and the locals knew that the spring would be a time of great danger. The exceptional amount of pack ice off the Spitsbergen coast meant that the area around Longyearben was recording an unusually high number of polar bears. Because of this, the local police had posted a large number of warning signs all over the town and at the airport. It should have been impossible for the two young students who arrived that spring to see the sights of the area to have missed the signs. It is a mystery how they would have been unaware of the danger. They went for a hike up Plataberget, a 1,575-foot-high mountain that rises from the valley in which Longyearben is situated, and in spite of all the publicity they were also unarmed. And then circumstances developed in an unforseen way.

They were attacked by a hungry young bear estimated at only sixteen months old. One of the girls, just 22, was killed immediately by savage bites to her neck and head. The other girl escaped, seemingly by hurling herself down a ravine, badly injuring her leg but somehow crawled back to Longyearbyen for help. About an hour after the horrific attack, the armed police finally found the grisly site of the kill. The bear was still lingering close to the bloody remains of the girl's dead body, protecting the carcass as food from other bears and the police marksmen had no alternative but to shoot it. But for one young tourist it was already much too late.

That was in the spring. But on the 1 September in the same year, on a small island, Kiepertoya, in the north-east of Svalbard, five members of the crew of a tourist ship went for a walk along the shore. They had some protection, but it was pathetically inadequate, a flare gun, a flare pen and a .22-calibre pistol. They spotted a large adult male polar bear about 80 yards away, coming towards them fast. They tried scaring it with flares but this had little or no effect. The bear attacked the group and two of the men stood their ground, and one attempted to shoot it with the pistol, firing several shots. The rest of the group ran away in terror. One man, a 58-year-old crew-member, was killed almost instantly by several vicious bites to the head. The other, a 49-year-old, somehow survived although he had one ear almost torn off, was bitten badly in the neck and had a vicious wound to one arm.

It was many hours later that the attack was reported in Longyearbyen and because it was clear that the bear was likely to have been injured by the pistol, the police raced to the island, found the bear and shot it. Post-mortem results showed that although the bear had been hit with several shots from the .22 pistol they had done little or no damage.

These are the last two recorded deaths from polar bears in Norway.

Twenty years ago or less Svalbard saw very few tourists, only scientists doing scientific research in the summer months. In recent years both tourism and scientific research have become year-round activities. This will inevitably result in more confrontations with bears and more human casualties. Anyone visiting this region must make sure they are suffi-ciently well armed and do nothing to provoke such a beautiful but deadly creature.

Visitors to the Arctic should heed the advice of the Inuit elders who believe that a polar bear can hear a person's thoughts. 'Don't think ill of polar bears' goes the old Inuit teaching – 'for that might make them angry … and you don't want to make them angry …'

Polar Bears killed in Svalbard 1998–2004

Date ymd	Place	Cause	Involved	Bear	Age
980206	Brandalspynten, Ny-Ålesund	PM	GO	Male	4–5
980410	Hopen	SD	C	Male	1–2
980808	G shamna, Hornsund	SD	T	Male	2
980809	G shamna, Hornsund	SD	T	Male	2-3
000614	Smeerenburgfjorden	AM	GO	Male	>5
000731	G shamna, Hornsund	SD	S	Female	7
000801	G shamna, Hornsund	AM/PM	GO	Male	1–2
000801	G shamna, Hornsund	AM/PM	GO	Female	1–2
010426	Bj rn ya	SD	C	Male	7
010702	Kapp Amsterdam, Sveagruva	PM	GO	Female	3
020710	Eholmen, Bellsund	SD	T	Male	9
020716	Colesbukta	PM	GO	Female	7
020716	Colesbukta	PM	GO	Male	1–2
020716	Colesbukta	PM	GO	Female	1–2
021207	Isbj rnhamna, Hornsund	SD	C	Male	2-3
030203	Austfjordneset	SD	C	Male	17
030513	Adventdalen	PM	GO	Male	3
030517	Mushamna	SD	C	Male	4–5
040224	Vestpynten	SD	T	Female	2
040510	Van Mijenfjorden	AM	GO	Male	0.5
040421	Van Keulenfjorden	Accident	S	Male	15
040609	Fridtjofhamna	Prosecuted	T	Male	2.5
041230	Barentsburg	PM	GO	Male	2

SD = self-defence; AM = act of mercy; PM = precautionary measure; GO = Govenor's office;
C = station crew; S = scientist; T = tourist

The Future of the Polar Bear

It's a proud achievement of conservation that, thanks to international law, polar bears are not registered at present as endangered.

But around the globe, increasing levels of greenhouse gas in the atmosphere are causing temperatures to rise. As a result, each year the Arctic sea ice now melts earlier and forms later. During the last five years in the Arctic there has been a 7 per cent reduction in ice cover and a 40 per cent loss in ice thickness. As their offshore habitat shrinks, polar bears in the southern limits of the Arctic, particularly in Canada around Hudson's Bay, face a grave threat to their survival. The bears need sea ice to hunt for food and to help them move from their hunting grounds to their denning or summer resting areas.

At the current rate of climate warming, however, it's predicted that by the year 2080 in Hudson's Bay there will be no ice at all. Indeed, inside this century it is possible that in the summer months the ice cover surrounding the North Pole itself will disappear completely. Not only would the polar bears suffer a profound effect from a shrinking habitat but also increased difficulty in hunting seals. In addition, polar bears need large volumes of solid snow in which to dig the dens for their cubs. Less ice also creates a danger that different populations of bears will become completely isolated from each other. Possibly in certain areas they will starve.

Another major threat to the bears is the fact that alarming levels of several comparatively new toxic compounds have been found in the Arctic. Polar bears and other large carnivores take in large quantities of these pollutants via the seals and fish that they live on. There has been evidence of some level of pollution in the Arctic for many years now but

It's predicted that by the year 2080 in Hudson's Bay there will be no ice at all. In this century it is possible that in the summer months the ice cover surrounding the North Pole will disappear completely.

A bear off the coast of Svalbard. The permanent ice is shrinking by 9 per cent each decade.

the development of modern synthetic chemicals is a new threat. These are believed to be pushed into the area by the wind and sea currents from Europe and Asia. Scientific research suggests that by being ingested into the blubber of polar bears, trace elements of these chemicals are enough to hamper the animals' immune system. This will increase susceptibility to parasites and disease. High levels of the same poisons have also been linked to reproductive failure and malformed organs. For example, some bears have been found in recent years with both male and female genitalia.

Polar bears in the southern limits of the Arctic face a grave threat to their survival. The bears need sea ice to hunt for food and to help them move from their hunting grounds to their summer resting areas. In certain areas they could starve.

A Mammal Conservation and Relocation helicopter at work.

The polar bear, being at the top of a food chain, suffers the most of all creatures in the Arctic ecosystem. Its cubs are in particular danger because they receive very high doses through their mother's milk.

In the Svalbard archipelago, for many years the Norwegian Polar Institute has been conducting a programme of research into polar bears. From the 1960s animals were tagged, and samples taken from many of the bears that had been killed by hunters. Today the research is done exclusively on live animals. Much of the field work is carried out using helicopter transport, which gives the researchers access to large numbers of bears over great expanses of territory.

On average about a hundred bears a year are captured and measured, giving data to be used in a variety of studies. From all the captured bears, blood and tissue samples are taken, and since 1990 more than a thousand bears have been marked and approximately a hundred females have been fitted with satellite transmitters, making it possible to see how much polar bears might be moving from one area to the other. The bears' movements can be tracked using collars fitted with a radio device. However, it is only the female that can be followed in this way – male bears actually have a neck wider than their head, which in either sex is relatively small compared to the body, so that in their case the collars would simply fall off.

At present the polar bear still knows no boundaries, and can happily pad across the icebound ocean from Russia to Alaska, from Canada to Greenland, and to northern Norway including the whole of the Svalbard archipelago. In the mean time, scientific knowledge contines to grow concerning the dangers that face this legendary creature. So too does worldwide public awareness of these hazards. Once already in recent times, with hunting outlawed by international consent, the polar bear has been rescued from near extinction by human intervention. Another similar effort, calling up the goodwill of people and organizations through many nations, is needed in our own time. Such an achievement would help ensure the survival, and the freedom to roam, of the Norsemens' rider of the iceberg, the Laplanders' God's dog, the Inuits' Nanuk, the creature who 'above all others deserves respect'.

At present the polar bear still knows no boundaries, and can happily pad across the icebound ocean from Russia to Alaska, from Canada to Greenland, to Norway.

The Inuit have a word for the emotion the sight of a polar bear evokes — iliyra — fear accompanied by awe.

We must protect the Norsemen's rider of the iceberg, the Laplanders' God's dog, the Inuits' Nanuk, the creature who above all others deserves respect.

WITH THANKS TO

James Hewlett – Norwegian Coastal Voyage
Rune B Hansen – Vice Governor, Svalbard
Erik Vike and the team at Spitsbergen Travel
Nina Bailey
Frigg Jorgensen
Martin & Jean Founds – Martin's World Travel
North Face for all the clothes that kept us warm
And the crew Dave, Geraint, Richard and Kim.

PICTURE CREDITS

All pictures © Nina Bailey/Norwegian Coastal Voyage,
except the following:

2 N Ovsyanikov/RSPCA Photolibrary
7 NHPA/B & C Alexander
8 Robert Henno / Still Pictures
8 Robert Henno / Still Pictures
11 Michio Hoshino/Minden Pictures/FLPA
12 M Watson/ardea.com
12 Fred Bruemmer / Still Pictures
15 Michio Hoshino/Minden Pictures/FLPA
16 Fred Bruemmer / Still Pictures
19 NHPA/B & C Alexander
20 Mark Newman/FLPA
23 Steven Kazlowski / Still Pictures
65 plainpicture/Kirch, S.
92 www.bluegreenpictures.com
107 Andrew Bannister/Getty Images
109 Doc White/ardea.com
110 Kenneth W Fink/ardea.com
112 M Rich-Griffith/RSPCA Photolibrary
116 Steve Bloom/stevebloom.com
119 Silvestris Fotoservice/FLPA
120 Fritz Polking/FLPA
122 NHPA/Kevin Schafer
126 Fritz Polking/FLPA
132 Michio Hoshino/Minden Pictures/FLPA
134 M Watson/ardea.com
137 M Watson/ardea.com
138 M Watson/ardea.com
140 M Watson/ardea.com
144 Frans Lanting/Minden Pictures/FLPA
147 Jim Brandenburg/Minden Pictures/FLPA
147 NHPA/B & C Alexander
148 NHPA/B & C Alexander
150 NHPA/Andy Rouse
153 NHPA/B & C Alexander
154 Mark Newman/FLPA
157 NHPA/Dan Griggs
157 NHPA/B & C Alexander

First published in the United Kingdom in 2005 by
Weidenfeld & Nicolson

Text copyright © Chris Tarrant 2005
Design and layout copyright © Weidenfeld & Nicolson
2005

The moral right of Chris Tarrant to be identified as the
author of this work has been asserted in accordance with
the Copyright, Design and Patents act of 1988.

Design: Grade Design Consultants, London
Editorial: Sue Webb, Jennie Condell, Jo Murray
Picture Research: Bronagh Woods

A CIP catalogue record for this book is available from the
British Library

ISBN 0-297-84422-9

Printed and bound in Italy

Weidenfeld & Nicolson
The Orion Publishing Group
Wellington House
125 Strand
London WC2R 0BB